In 1802, William Wordsworth married Mary Hutchinson, and he and his wife and sister continued to live together at Dove Cottage. Dorothy Wordsworth wrote in her journal: 'On Monday 4th October 1802, my brother William was married to Mary Hutchinson. I slept a good deal of the night and rose fresh and well in the morning. At a little after 8 o'clock I saw them go down the avenue towards the Church. William had parted from me upstairs. I gave him the wedding ring – with how deep a blessing! I took it from my forefinger where I had worn it the whole of the night before – he slipped it again onto my little finger and blessed me fervently. When they were absent my dear little Sara prepared the breakfast. I kept myself as quiet as I could, but when I saw the two men running up the walk, coming to tell us it was over, I could stand it no longer and threw myself on the bed where I lay in stillness, neither hearing or seeing anything, till Sara came upstairs to me and said, "They are coming." This forced me from the bed where I lay and I moved I knew not how straight forward, faster than my strength could carry me till I met my beloved William and fell upon his bosom.'

Also in this series in Granada Paperbacks

Welsh Walks and Legends
by Showell Styles
(Illustrated)

West Country Walks and Legends
by J. H. N. Mason
(Illustrated)

Brian J. Bailey

Lakeland
Walks and Legends

A MAYFLOWER BOOK

GRANADA
London Toronto Sydney New York

Published by Granada Publishing Limited in 1981

ISBN 0 583 13249 9

A Granada Paperbacks UK Original
Copyright © Brian J. Bailey 1981

Granada Publishing Limited
Frogmore, St Albans, Herts AL2 2NF
and
3 Upper James Street, London W1R 4BP
866 United Nations Plaza, New York, NY 10017, USA
117 York Street, Sydney, NSW 2000, Australia
100 Skyway Avenue, Rexdale, Ontario, M9W 3A6, Canada
PO Box 84165, Greenside, 2034 Johannesburg, South Africa
61 Beach Road, Auckland, New Zealand

Set, printed and bound in Great Britain by
Cox & Wyman Ltd, Reading
Filmset in Linotype Plantin

Granada ®
Granada Publishing ®

80 012716

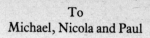

To
Michael, Nicola and Paul

ACKNOWLEDGMENTS

The photographs on pages 39, 88, 92, 111, 126 and 163, are by my old friend V. K. Guy. I am also deeply indebted to Vic, and to Pauline, for their generous hospitality during my researches.

I am indebted to Alberto Sciama of Pictor International Ltd, for his kindness in allowing me to reproduce the picture of Dent on page 156.

The photograph on page 77 of Greta Hall in Keswick is by kind permission of the British Tourist Authority.

The other photographs are my own. Without the hard work and companionship of my wife, I doubt that it would have been possible for me to write this book at all.

CONTENTS

INTRODUCTION

When Daniel Defoe visited the Lake District during his tour through the 'Whole Island of Great Britain', he was struck by the 'inhospitable terror' of the mountains. 'Here we entered Westmoreland,' he wrote, 'a country eminent only for being the wildest, most barren and frightful of any that I have passed over in England, or even in Wales itself.'

It is hardly an opinion we should endorse today, but even Wordsworth, the greatest champion of Lakeland beauty, had experienced the intimidating effect of the mountains on occasions, referring in 'The Prelude' to a 'huge cliff' which

> 'Rose up between me and the stars, and still,
> With measured motion, like a living thing,
> Strode after me.'

In an area that once seemed, particularly to outsiders, remote, forbidding and desolate, we should expect a unique folklore to have grown up among the sparse and benighted population, but in fact Cumberland and Westmorland were not so strange. They had been penetrated by Celts, Romans and Vikings, and their names and legends – to say nothing of their language – derive largely from those influences. Common words like fell, gill, beck, scree and tarn are of Norse origin, and they indicate the slightly abrasive character of the local dialect.

It is only recently that the English Lake District has come to be recognized as a unified whole. Until the twelfth century, Cumberland belonged to the Scottish kingdom of Strathclyde, and then, even after the Lake District became the first of Britain's National Parks, it was split up between Lancashire, Cumberland and Westmorland until 1974, when the Local Government Act united this splendid region into the new county of Cumbria.

I have attempted in this book to tell a wide variety of Lakeland stories from all over the region, beginning with a princess in the east and ending with another in the west. They will provide the reader with a sense of local life and history and, if he follows many of the walks, he will also see much of the finest scenery. About half the stories are 'legends' in the strict sense, but nearly all the others, though true, are concerned with 'legendary' Lake District characters. In a few cases, each reader must decide for himself where truth ends and legend begins, and there is even a spot of what might be called 'midsummer madness' here and there.

The walks described are intended for the average visitor and his family who are prepared to leave the blessed car for a while and enjoy Lakeland on foot at a leisurely pace. Climbing and fell-walking are not touched upon. No one should attempt the Lake District peaks without proper instruction, suitable clothing and capable physical condition.

I have given the approximate distance of each walk assuming the use of a car to a suitable starting point. Each walk brings you back to your parking place, and I have given National Grid references to these so that they can be found on any Ordnance Survey map of the region. If you do not have the use of a car, many of the starting points can be reached by public transport. The length of the walks varies from short strolls to around eight miles, but the majority are quite short and easy so that children can do them too.

One or two of the walks are by surfaced roadways, but wear sensible footwear for all of them, bearing in mind that wet ground is often likely to be encountered in Cumbria. After all, the Lake District would not be the Lake District if it were not wet, but do not be discouraged. Lakeland weather is itself legendary – it can change suddenly and dramatically, and is often exhilarating. You can sometimes stand beside the shore of Windermere at Bowness and watch rain clouds scudding towards you across Langdale Pikes, obscuring the mountains, and within minutes you can see sheets of rain sweeping across the opposite shores of the lake. But by the time you have put on your raincoat and fastened it, the sky has cleared again, and the sunlight picks out the distant peaks and makes the surface of the water shimmer, while to the north-east you may behold the most brilliant and spectacular rainbow forming a perfect bridge over the landscape.

In exploring Cumbria, remember that, although so much of it is a National Park, and a great deal is owned by the National Trust, it is still a working part of Britain, where the inhabitants depend for their livelihood on farming as well as the tourist trade. I have not tediously catalogued every single gate that you will meet on your walks, because where the route is unambiguous, you may pass through them, but never leave them open, or damage dry-stone walls, or leave litter, or allow your dog to harass sheep. By observing simple courtesy and common sense, you will be helping to protect this most beautiful corner of England from a fate worse than death.

WINDERMERE AND ESTHWAITE WATER

The Princess of Finsthwaite

The Crier of Claife

Jemima Puddle-Duck and Friends

The Skulls of Calgarth Hall

The Giants of Troutbeck

The Kirk Stone

1. THE PRINCESS OF FINSTHWAITE

In the churchyard at Finsthwaite, near the southern end of Windermere, is a white cross marking the grave of Clementina Johannes Sobieski Douglass, who was buried there in May 1771. The identity of this lady is one of the unsolved riddles of British history.

James Edward Stuart, the 'Old Pretender' to the Stuart line of succession, married in 1719 Maria Clementina Sobieski, grand-daughter of John III, King of Poland. In the following year she gave birth to a son in Rome, and he was soon to become known to the world as 'Bonnie Prince Charlie' – the 'Young Pretender'.

In 1745 the handsome and reckless twenty-five-year-old Charles came from France and landed in Scotland with seven companions, to raise a Jacobite rebellion and win a kingdom. He raised his standard at Glenfinnan and set forth to invade England with an army of about 6000 men, having drawn to his cause such eminent clansmen as Macleans, MacGregors, MacDonalds, Stewarts and Camerons. The tartan army crossed the border on 8 November, and after a five-day's siege, Charles rode into Carlisle on a white horse, preceded by a hundred kilted pipers.

Gathering reinforcements at Manchester, Charles marched towards London, but when he reached Derby, news of English armies numbering 30,000 men waiting to fall on his troops forced him to turn back. At Clifton Moor, south of Penrith, a rearguard action was fought against the forces of the Duke of Cumberland, which is often referred to as the last battle on English soil, though it was hardly more than a skirmish. In the following spring, the Young Pretender's dreams of glory were finally shattered by his crushing defeat at Culloden, and the fugitive Charles, with a price of £30,000 on his head, escaped to France in disillusion.

Everyone knows the story of the heroine Flora MacDonald, who aided the escape of the Prince by taking him to Skye disguised as her maid, but the lady buried in Finsthwaite churchyard may have been Bonnie Prince Charlie's daughter, born when he still had hopes of winning the English crown for his father.

At a house called Waterside, on the banks of the River Leven near Newby Bridge, the lady in question is said to have arrived as an infant, around 1746, with two servants, to live with the Taylor family there, who were Catholics and Jacobite sympathizers.

We must now go back twenty years, for in 1726, an officer in the Old Pretender's army, one John Walkenshawe, became a father, and named his daughter Clementina after James Edward's Polish wife, who was the child's godmother. When Clementina Walkenshawe grew up, she happened to be staying with relatives in Scotland when Bonnie Prince Charlie fell ill after his victory over the English at Falkirk. Clementina, who had known Charles since their childhood in Rome, nursed him, and probably became his mistress then.

She joined him on the Continent after his escape, and gave birth to a daughter Charlotte in 1754, but we do not know for certain if this was her first child. It is possible that she had borne Charles an earlier daughter, who was put in the care of supporters at Finsthwaite, and who was known locally as 'the Princess'. Her uncompromising names lay claim to descent from both the Stuart and the Polish royal lines, for 'Douglass' was the incognito Bonnie Prince Charlie travelled under. Clementina Walkenshawe asserted that Charles had made her his wife, but the truth of that is not known. At any rate, the claimant did not survive her twenty-fifth year.

Charles married Princess Louise of Stolberg in 1772, and spent six unhappy and childless years with her before she left him to enter a convent. He, nearing sixty, a broken-down and dissolute drunkard with no country, was cared for by his

The grave of 'Princess' Clementina Douglass at Finsthwaite.

daughter Charlotte as he drifted aimlessly from court to court, sponging on the Catholic princes of Europe, until his death in 1788.

We may never know for certain whether Finsthwaite churchyard really does contain a royal grave, but if Clementina Douglass *was* the legitimate daughter of Bonnie Prince Charlie, it is an interesting thought that if the '45 Rebellion had been successful, she might have lived to be Queen of England. Engraved at the foot of the gravestone are the words: 'Behold thy king cometh.'

THE WALK:
FINSTHWAITE AND NEWBY
BRIDGE

MAP SQUARE: E5
National Grid Ref: SD 368879
About 3 miles. Easy.

Park in Finsthwaite village and see the grave marked by a white cross in the churchyard. Walk back to the village street and, turning left, go along the road until you come to a bridle path on the left signposted to Newby Bridge. Follow this through the woods until it brings you to the road, crossing a railway line. This is the privately owned Haverthwaite and Lakeside Railway, where some steam locomotives are preserved, and round the sharp bend in the road to the left, you pass the diminutive station. Continue along the road and turn left before the road crosses the River Leven at Newby Bridge. The road crosses the railway line again then goes parallel with the lakeside, passing the railway terminus before turning uphill away from the lake. Keep left at the next two junctions and you are soon back at your car in Finsthwaite.

2. THE CRIER OF CLAIFE

Across the narrow waist of Windermere, at one of its shallowest parts, a regular ferry service carries cars and caravans to link the road between Kendal and Hawkshead. It is hardly more than a quarter of a mile across the lake at this point, from the Nab on the east bank to the Ferry House on the west, passing between Windermere's group of islands, the largest of which is Belle Isle.

Claife Heights, looking across Windermere from Bowness.

The crossing on the modern diesel-engined ferry is an easy and interesting one, from which the lake can be seen to advantage, and if you travel from the Bowness side, you can see on the opposite bank the beautiful and heavily wooded slopes of Claife Heights rising above the lake. The local agriculturalist John Curwen began the cultivation of larch on these hills at the end of the eighteenth century, and Wordsworth took exception to it, seeing no beauty in these foreign conifers.

Before the days of the motor-ferry, when ferrymen took travellers across the lake by rowing boat, the Claife Heights were much feared, for on them dwelt the Crier of Claife who, like the maiden of the Lorelei and the Sirens of Greek legend, lured boatmen and passengers to their deaths by the eerie power of his voice.

One ferryman rowed across the lake in response to wild cries of 'Boat! Boat!' from the other side, and returned speechless with horror and in a state of collapse, dying before he could tell anyone what had happened. In 1635, forty-seven people returning from a wedding at Hawkshead were drowned in a ferry accident for which the ghostly Crier was for long afterwards held responsible, and other deaths in ferry incidents were put down to the same evil influence.

Eventually a priest was called in to exorcize the troubled spirit, and as far as is known the Crier of Claife was heard no more, but if you should happen to hear strange cries from the western bank on a dark and stormy night, do not be tempted to cross, for you never know . . ,

THE WALK:
OVER CLAIFE HEIGHTS

MAP SQUARE: E4
National Grid Ref: SD 379955
About 6 miles. Fairly steep climb at first, but steady descent and level return. May be wet in places.

Cross Windermere by the ferry from Bowness, and proceed along the road to the car park a little way up on the right. A few yards back down the road towards the ferry, a signposted footpath leads off left to Claife Heights over a stone stile in the wall. The path twists and turns following a clearly waymarked route up the hillside and through woods. As it starts to descend, you reach the area from which the ghostly cries used to be heard, and the path makes a wide swing towards the lakeside at Belle Grange Bay and the prominent

Bass Rock, and joins the shore road there. Turn right on to this and return along the lakeside, passing the group of islands, and soon you reach the ferry road again, where you turn right to get back to the car park.

3. JEMIMA PUDDLE-DUCK AND FRIENDS

It was in 1908 when Jemima Puddle-Duck, wearing a shawl and a poke bonnet, first set out at Hill Top Farm to look for a secret nesting-place near the bottom of the farmyard, and found what seemed an ideal spot under the rhubarb leaves.

The farmhouse was at one end of the village of Sawrey, in Lancashire, behind an inn called the Tower Bank Arms, and the village and farm were soon familiar territory to many thousands of children who had never been to the Lake District.

Beatrix Potter, the creator of Jemima, Peter Rabbit, Squirrel Nutkin and many other famous characters of children's fiction, was born in London, but the family often spent holidays in Lakeland, and Beatrix grew to love the district so much that she bought Hill Top Farm, and eventually lived there.

Though her name is known the world over for her animal stories, the author herself was hardly known at all and – as with most creators of innocence – there was more to Miss Potter than met the eye. She was the daughter of a Victorian couple who had made their fortunes out of the Lancashire cotton trade. She was never sent to school, but was taught by governesses, and she had a lonely and very private childhood, in those days when a child was definitely not to speak unless spoken to. Her defence against this isolation came in the creation of a secret code, with which the growing girl kept a *Journal* over a period of sixteen years, and which was not deciphered until 1966.

Beatrix Potter's first animal story was about 'four little rabbits, whose names were Flopsy, Mopsy, Cottontail and Peter'. She wrote it in a letter to a sick child, and out of that developed her first book, *The Tale of Peter Rabbit*. Out of the proceeds of her books she bought Hill Top Farm and, in due course, much more property in the vicinity, and many of the stories and the water-colour drawings she made to illustrate them have recognizable Lake District locations. Hill Top Farm itself features in *The Tale of Jemima Puddle-Duck*; the village shop in *Ginger and Pickles*; St Herbert's Island, in Derwent Water, is the Owl Island where Squirrel Nutkin lost his tail; and Bull Banks, above the farm, is where Peter Rabbit tried to rescue Benjamin's family from the gruesome lair of Mr Tod, the fox.

In 1913, at the age of forty-seven, Beatrix Potter married her solicitor, William Heelis, and she settled down to become a farmer, with a special interest in breeding Herdwick sheep. At the same time, her literary output more or less dried up. Her marriage was a very happy one, and perhaps she had at last escaped from that private world of her childhood which had continued through her secret journal and her animals.

Beatrix Potter's house at Near Sawrey.

At any rate, she soon became not only a practical and successful farmer but also a public benefactor. She bought more and more property, always with an eye on the preservation of the Lake District's natural beauty. She gave much of her property to the National Trust during her lifetime, and when she died, in 1943, she left the Trust her home, which is opened to the public during the summer months.

THE WALK: MAP SQUARE: E5
AROUND NEAR SAWREY   National Grid Ref: SD 369957
                                       Short stroll at will. Easy.

A visit to Hill Top Farm can be made for its own sake, or combined with the previous walk. A pleasant alternative, however, is to walk down the village street after visiting the house, and turn left down the road that leads to Esthwaite Water, and walk round the west side of the lake. You can walk to Hawkshead by this road if you wish – a distance of about five miles there and back.

4. THE SKULLS OF CALGARTH HALL

On the eastern shore of Windermere, three miles from Ambleside, stood the large mansion known as Calgarth Hall, the seat of a powerful local family – the Philipsons. The story is told that one of the Philipsons, Myles by name, had designs on a property owned by a respectable old married couple named Cook, who lived nearby. Unable to obtain the estate by lawful means, it is said, he invited the couple to a party at the Hall and then got them convicted on a trumped-up charge of theft, for which they were duly executed, but not before Dorothy Cook had put a curse on the Philipsons and their house.

The monstrous Philipson was soon made to regret his ill-gotten gain, for the skulls of the old couple came to Calgarth to haunt him. They suddenly appeared, after the execution, in a niche on the staircase, and of course the master of the house gave instructions for them to be removed, and they were buried. Soon afterwards, however, they were seen to be in the niche as before, so they were thrown in the lake, but again they appeared in the house soon afterwards. Now the master of the house attempted to rid himself of this vengeful spectre by having the pair of skulls burnt to a cinder once and for all. The order having been carried out, the skulls nevertheless reappeared on the shelf from which they had evidently chosen to remind the Philipsons for ever of their wicked deed.

By now, the master's alarm was clear, if the legend is to be believed, for he next had the two skulls ground to powder. But this remedy had no more effect than the previous ones, for still the skulls were seen, whole and defiant, on the staircase, and it is said that many people saw them before the Hall passed into the possession of Bishop Watson, who had the niche walled up with the skulls inside.

The Philipsons and their house having long ago passed away, the Cooks' vengeance is complete, and though the story is still remembered, no one is troubled any more by the ghostly skulls of Calgarth.

THE WALK:
ORREST HEAD

MAP SQUARE: E4
National Grid Ref: SD 413987
A little over a mile. Steady climb and descent, with a little care needed near the top, but well worth the effort.

The Calgarth estate (where flying-boats were built during the Second World War) is privately owned, and there is nothing of interest to see there now, but Orrest Head rises behind it and more than compensates for the omission.

From Windermere Station, walk along the main road towards Ambleside for a few yards, and turn right along the signposted and surfaced path near the Youth Hostel Association's regional office. Simply follow this winding path on its route up through the woods,

The view across Windermere from above the Calgarth estate.

26

past the Woodman's Cottage, until the tarmac ends at a fork where you bear right on the rough track. This brings you to the open ground at the top of the hill.

The view from here is certainly one of the finest in the Lake District. A chart at the top explains the details of the panorama before you, which includes Windermere, Scafell Pike (14 miles away), Bowfell and Great Gable, Coniston Old Man and the Langdale Pikes, and in the opposite direction, Shap Fells and the Pennines. Descend by the same route.

5. THE GIANTS OF TROUTBECK

It may surprise you to know that the village of Troutbeck, which lies above Windermere between the lake and the Kirkstone Pass, has long been famous for breeding giants. They were such men as Hugh Heard and Great Will of the Tarns, and although they do not appear in *The Guinness Book of Records*, their exploits have been recounted from generation to generation in the district.

Hugh Heard was known as both archer and wrestler – 'a man of prodigious strength and stature' – who wreaked havoc among the marauding bands of Scotsmen who sometimes invaded the territory. He once told the king, on being asked about his diet, that he normally had thick pottage and cream for breakfast and a whole sheep for dinner, but he would sometimes go for days after such a meal without eating at all. One account says that his mother had been a nun in Furness Abbey, thrown out when she appeared pregnant. Hugh was quite capable of lifting a thirty-foot oak beam, but it is said that he died at the age of forty-two through pulling up trees by the roots.

If Great Will of the Tarns had any stockings to fit him, he stood nine feet six in his stockinged feet. He was known in the neighbourhood as a fine labourer and a formidable adversary to the Scottish raiders.

One evening, Lady Eva le Fleming of Coniston Hall was walking beside the lake, attended by her maid, Barbara. Suddenly the giant sprang out in front of them, grabbed the helpless maid as if she were a rag doll, and made off into the woods with the shrieking female under his arm. The terrified Lady Eva ran back to the hall and breathlessly told what had happened, whereupon the menfolk instantly set off in pursuit of the giant, some on foot and others on horseback. Among them was Dick Hawksley, the lord's falconer, whom Barbara apparently held in some affection.

The posse caught up with Great Will near Cauldron Dub, and realizing he could not escape them, the giant angrily hurled his screaming victim into the flooded beck and raced on. Hawksley plunged into the water to rescue the damsel in distress, but although he managed to seize and hold on to her, the current of the flood waters was too strong for him, and the gallant lad and his lover were swept away, their bodies being washed up some days later.

Meanwhile, the others had pursued the giant until he collapsed beneath a rain of blows from their swords, and Great Will died with blood running from a hundred wounds.

A farmyard at Troutbeck.

THE WALK:	MAP SQUARE: E4
THROUGH TROUTBECK	National Grid Ref: NY 409032
VILLAGE	2 miles. Easy. May be a little wet in places.

Troutbeck is a delightful street village of grey stone and slate with whitewashed houses and numerous wells, some of which bear the names of saints. The Trout Beck from which the village takes its name is quite a long river flowing south beside the village and into Windermere via the Calgarth estate. Giants are not noticeably common in Troutbeck today, but the village is well worthy of attention.

Drive along the A592 north from Windermere until you cross the beck by Church Bridge, then past the church and the Queen's Head on the left. Take the very tight turn next left, with great care round the awkward uphill corner, and drive to the village centre to park in the vicinity of the Post Office.

Continue down the street on foot, and just before you reach the Y-junction, on the right is Town End, a fine seventeenth-century yeoman's house, with mullioned windows, now owned by the National Trust, and open for visitors in summer (the house, not the windows). Having seen this, walk back towards the Post Office and turn right down the hill, following the lane over the stream until you reach the church on the main road. The church is much restored, but it has stained-glass windows by William Morris and Burne-Jones, and the panelling in the stalls came from Calgarth Hall.

Just past the church on the left is a footpath, and a few yards along it, on the right, is a gate with a stile beside it. Go over this and through the field to the corner of a fence, then straight ahead to the group of trees and through two kissing gates along the left side of a fence until another gate by a wall takes you up to a signposted crossroads. The road ahead is now surfaced past the Mortal Man Hotel (don't miss reading the inn sign!), and at the junction with the village street you turn left to return to your car.

6. THE KIRK STONE

Kirkstone Pass, the road between Windermere and Ullswater, is nearly 1500 feet above sea-level at its highest point, and the modern road, having little option in the matter, follows the course of the medieval pack-horse road – not an outstanding example of civil engineering!

> 'He surely is an arrant ass
> Who pays to ride up Kirkstone Pass.
> He'll find in spite of all their talking,
> He'll have to walk, and pay for walking.'

So wrote a traveller in the days of the stage-coach, and not for nothing does the road up to the pass from Ambleside rejoice in the name of 'The Struggle', having a gradient of one in four in places. The innkeeper at Ambleside would not, according to De Quincey, 'mount this formidable hill without four horses', and De Quincey himself, preparing to accompany the Wordsworths on an expedition, 'took it for granted that we were to walk; however, at the moment of starting, a cart – the common farmer's cart of the country – made its appearance; and the driver was a bonny young woman of the vale. Such a vehicle I had never in my life seen used for such a purpose; but what was good enough for the Wordsworths was good enough for me.'

So the ascent began, but soon 'all riding in a cart drawn by one horse becomes impossible'. If the climb could be alarming, however, the descent could be worse, especially with a woman driver. 'In utter darkness,' gasps De Quincey, 'after midnight, and the darkness irradiated only by continual streams of lightning, I was driven down this whole descent, at a full gallop, by a young woman . . .'

A four-foot-high rock near the summit has long been fancied to resemble the steep roof of a Scandinavian church,

The Kirkstone Pass, with Brothers Water beyond.

and Wordsworth, in his *Ode to the Pass of Kirkstone*, refers to the rock 'whose Church-like frame / Gives to the savage pass its name'.

The word 'kirk', of course, comes from the Old Norse for church, 'kirkja', and it occurs often in Cumbria. When the inn at the top of the pass was being built, however, in 1840, an ancient burial mound was discovered, and as 'kirk' was used also to describe a mound, or heap of stones, it is possible that this was the origin of the name.

At any rate, a trip over Kirkstone Pass is still a rewarding experience on a clear day, and still a slightly alarming one in bad weather.

THE WALK:	MAP SQUARE: E4
TO THE KIRK STONE	National Grid Ref: NY 401081
	A little less than a mile. Easy.

The A592 road from Windermere is an easier drive than 'The Struggle' from Ambleside, which joins it just before the Kirkstone

Pass Inn is reached. Park just past the inn on the right and look back for a view of Ambleside and Windermere. Walk along the roadside away from Windermere, and two hundred yards from the inn you reach the highest point of the pass, 1476 feet. This is the highest motor road in Lakeland. The unmistakable Kirk Stone is on the left, with Red Screes towering above (these give a good echo if you feel inclined to shout). Continue down the road to the bend until you reach the car park on the left, and admire the view of Brothers Water from here. Then return to your car and continue by engine-power.

GRASMERE AND RYDAL WATER
Wordsworth Country

7. WORDSWORTH COUNTRY

William Wordsworth and his sister Dorothy, the most famous natives of Lakeland, were born at Cockermouth, but although there is scarcely a corner of the Lake District that does not have Wordsworth associations, it is to Grasmere and Rydal that all roads lead when the Wordsworths are under discussion.

William went to school in Hawkshead and then to Cambridge, after which he spent some time in France and became a supporter of the Revolution. Then after a few years in the south of England, he and Dorothy set up house together at Dove Cottage, Grasmere.

Wordsworth always loved travelling, but the Lake District remained his permanent home for the rest of his life. In 1802, he married Mary Hutchinson, and he and his wife and sister continued to live together at Dove Cottage. Dorothy recorded the wedding day in her journal: 'On Monday, 4 October 1802, my Brother William was married to Mary Hutchinson. I slept a good deal of the night and rose fresh and well in the morning. At a little after eight o'clock I saw them go down the avenue towards the Church. William had parted from me upstairs. I gave him the wedding ring – with how deep a blessing! I took it from my forefinger where I had worn it the whole of the night before – he slipped it again onto my finger and blessed me fervently. When they were absent my dear little Sara prepared the breakfast. I kept myself as quiet as I could, but when I saw the two men running up the walk, coming to tell us it was over, I could stand it no longer and threw myself on the bed where I lay in stillness, neither hearing or seeing anything, till Sara came upstairs to me and said "They are coming." This forced me from the bed where I lay and I moved I knew not how straight forward, faster than my strength could carry me till I met my beloved William and fell upon his bosom.'

In 1805 Wordsworth's brother John was drowned at

Weymouth, and the shock had a profound physical and mental effect on William who, at the age of thirty-nine, was taken for a man of sixty, according to Thomas De Quincey. Some time later, two of his children died. Little wonder that Benjamin Haydon, the painter, described Wordsworth's head 'as if it was carved out of a mossy rock, created before the flood,' and Sir Henry Taylor referred to his 'hard weather-beaten old face . . . full of rifts and clefts and fissures, out of which, someone said, you might expect lichens to grow'.

In 1808 the trio had moved to Allan Bank, where for a time they provided a roof for Coleridge, De Quincey and Coleridge's children, as well as for William's and Mary's own infants. This arrangement did not last long. The Wordsworths then spent two years at the Rectory, Grasmere, after which they moved to Rydal Mount, William having by then been appointed Stamp Distributor for Westmorland, which provided him with a small salary.

A family servant told Canon Rawnsley how difficult it was to get Wordsworth to leave his study when dinner was served. Sometimes they had to resort to dropping a dish or a bottle outside his door. 'Eh dear, that maistly wad bring him out, wad that. It was nobbut that as wad, howivver. For ye kna that he was a verra careful man, and he couldn't do with brekking t'china.'

Dorothy had made a typical entry in her journal on 30 April 1802: 'We came into the orchard directly after Breakfast, and sate there. The lake was calm – the sky cloudy. We saw two fishermen by the lake side. William began to write the poem of the Celandine. I wrote to Mary H. sitting on the fur gown. Walked backwards and forwards with William – he repeated his poem to me. Then he got to work again and could not give over – he had not finished his dinner till five o'clock . . .'

William lived at Rydal Mount with his family for the rest of his life. He became a local JP and was given various honours,

Rydal Water.

culminating in his appointment as Poet Laureate in 1843, succeeding Robert Southey. The locals accepted him as a 'decent quiet man'. Some thought him a bit mad, but he was a typical Northerner, 'rough feaced' and 'vara plaainly drest at best o' times'. One man, attracted to a political meeting by the announcement that the Poet Laureate was to speak, left in disgust when he discovered that it was 'nobbut old Wudswuth o' Rydal efter aw'. Some of the locals assumed after his death that Wordsworth's son would 'carry on the business'.

William Wordsworth died at Rydal Mount in 1850, a few days after his eightieth birthday. Apart from his poetry, he was the author of what is perhaps still the best guide to the Lake District, in which he anticipated the conservation of the region as a National Park, but later on he was a fierce opponent of the railways and the tourist invasion: 'The directors of railway companies are always ready to devise or encourage entertainments for tempting the humbler classes to leave their homes. Accordingly, for the profit of the shareholders and that of the lower class of innkeepers, we should have wrestling matches, horse and boat races without number, and pot-houses and beer-shops would keep pace with these excitements and recreations, most of which might too easily be had elsewhere. The injury which would thus be done to morals, both among this influx of strangers and the lower class of inhabitants, is obvious, and supposing such extraordinary temptations not to be held out, there cannot be a doubt that the Sabbath day in the towns of Bowness and Ambleside, and other parts of the district, would be subject to much additional desecration.'

Wordsworth was always a formidable walker. He ascended Helvellyn when he was in his seventies, and during his wanderings, often accompanied by his sister, much of his finest nature poetry was conceived. But those who only know Wordsworth as a daffodil fancier should explore his poetry as well as his homes. He was a man with a powerful and original mind and wide-ranging sympathies who – according to his own testimony – thought twelve hours about society for every one about poetry.

> 'Thus often would he leave our peaceful home,
> And find elsewhere his business or delight;
> Out of our Valley's limits did he roam:
> Full many a time, upon a stormy night,
> His voice came to us from the neighbouring height:
> Oft could we see him driving in full view
> At mid-day when the sun was shining bright;
> What ill was on him, what he had to do,
> A mighty wonder bred among our quiet crew.'

THE WALK: GRASMERE AND RYDAL

MAP SQUARE: E4
National Grid Ref: NY 337075
About 4 miles. Easy, but allow plenty of time if you want to see the Wordsworth homes, etc.

Park in Grasmere village and leave by crossing the river beyond the church, going towards Town End. The minor road on the far side of the junction with the Ambleside road is the old Wishing Gate Road, and beside it is Dove Cottage and the Wordsworth Museum, both of which can be visited during the summer except Sundays. Thomas De Quincey lived at Dove Cottage after Wordsworth. Continue along the minor road, which follows a roughly semicircular route round the hillside. The so-called Wishing Gate is about halfway round on the right, and there is a beautiful view of Grasmere from it. Farther round, the minor road joins the main road again. Walk along this beside Rydal Water, passing Nab Cottage on the left, where Hartley Coleridge and De Quincey lived for a time. Soon you come into Rydal village, and turning left past the church, Rydal Mount is about two hundred yards up the hill. It is open daily. The garden was laid out by Wordsworth. Turn left on the narrow lane past the house, through the gate, and continue along the footpath, going along to the right of a wall, and glimpsing Rydal Water through the trees. Keep going on a more or less straight course, through the gates and over two or three streams, until bearing left you come back to the road again. Turn right and proceed to the junction and back to Grasmere. As you reach the church, you may like to see the simple graves of the Wordsworths in the far corner of the churchyard, with that of Hartley Coleridge nearby.

CONISTON WATER

The Drunken Duck
and other Dozy Animals

The Old Man of Coniston

8. THE DRUNKEN DUCK
AND OTHER DOZY ANIMALS

The first time I visited the Lake District, about twenty-five years ago, I stayed in the house of an amiable couple at Coniston. The husband worked in one of the local quarries. His wife prepared a meal for when he came home in the evenings, and afterwards, if I was not going anywhere, we sat round the fire and talked. One night he told me the story of how the 'Drunken Duck Inn', near Hawkshead, got its name, for it had formerly been known as 'Barngates Inn', and indeed was still marked as such on an Ordnance Survey map I had.

It seems that the innkeeper kept a few ducks, and one day, when a beer barrel burst in the yard, the ducks drank the ale and collapsed in a drunken stupor. When the innkeeper saw the birds, he thought they were dead, and asked his wife to pluck them ready for cooking, which she did. She got the fright of her life when the naked ducks awoke from their slumber. The ducks themselves were rather startled, too, no doubt. She could hardly let them loose again in that vulnerable condition, so she sat down and knitted woollen pullovers to keep them warm until they could grow new feathers.

Well, pulling wool over the eyes is a traditional Cumbrian pastime, but what I can tell you for a fact is that the farmers and shepherds of this district used to have a dialect counting system for checking their sheep, which went roughly as follows (there were slight regional variations): yan, tan, tethera, methéra, pimp, sethera, lethera, hovera, dovera, dick, yan-a-dick, tan-a-dick, tethera-dick, and so on.

Now young children in Cumbrian schools – like the rest of us – spent their time learning Standard English, even if they wanted to be farmers or shepherds when they grew up, so the time came when they had to be taught to count in dialect, and being practical men, the Cumbrian farmers chose the time for these exercises very shrewdly. They took the youngsters among the Herdwicks when it was 'clipping' time, and had the budding shepherds counting up to a hundred, over and over again, out loud. They were naturally rather slow and hesitant at first, and you can imagine the drone: 'Yan . . . tan . . . tethera . . . er . . . methera . . . pimp . . . er . . . sethera, lethera . . .' and so on, *ad nauseam*.

After about an hour of all this, the sheep (not to mention the scholars) fell into a deep slumber, and the waiting shearers then moved in, their task having been made much easier by this ingenious local device for killing two birds with one stone.

To return to the duckpond, however, one of the favourite stories in the Dales concerns a sportsman who was going home after an abysmal day's shooting. He came to a farm where an old farmer was standing by a gate watching a lot of tame ducks on the pond. 'How much do you want for just one shot at those ducks?' asked the frustrated sportsman, his eyes lighting up at the prospect of a bag at last.

'Five bob!' said the farmer. The sportsman instantly nodded his agreement, took careful aim, fired both barrels, and bagged a few ducks.

'I reckon I had the best of that bargain,' he said, with a satisfied grin, as he paid his five shillings.

'Oh I wouldn't say that,' said the old man. 'Them's not *my* ducks!'

THE WALK:	MAP SQUARE: E4
HAWKSHEAD AND TARN	National Grid Ref: SD 353981
HOWS	About 6 miles. Steady climb and descent.

Park in Hawkshead and spend half an hour before or after the walk looking round this charming and picturesque village with its narrow lanes and quaint cottages. Turn up the lane opposite the Red Lion until you see a signpost directing you to The Tarns, right. The lane brings you to a footpath across the fields, crossing Penrose

Beck and another lane at right angles, after which you reach the main road. Go left until you reach the Baptist Chapel at Hawkshead Hill on the right, and fork right by the telephone box. Continue along this road, ignoring the turns off it either side. There are splendid views near the top and soon you come to the tarn itself, which has been formed from a number of smaller pools by means of a dam. From the left side of the lake as you approach it, follow the footpath down along the right side of a stream to the main road at Glen Mary Bridge and, turning left, leave the road again almost immediately, where it turns right, by means of a lane off to the left. This soon joins the Coniston road through woodland. Turn left at the T-junction and follow the winding road until you come back to the Baptist Chapel. A little farther on retrace your steps across the fields to Hawkshead.

A corner of Hawkshead.

But you have not yet, you may complain, seen the 'Drunken Duck'. Drive along the Ambleside road from Hawkshead for about a mile, and bear left at the Y-junction where there is a public *telephone box. You will find the inn at the next crossroads. Turn right here, and at the T-junction you can either turn left for Ambleside, or right to get back to Hawkshead.*

9. THE OLD MAN OF CONISTON

The title above is given to the mountain rising behind
Coniston village, west of the lake, but the name is probably a
corruption of the Celtic 'alt maen' meaning 'high crag'. The
human association one expects of the name surely belongs on
the opposite bank of Coniston Water, where John Ruskin
lived and died.

Ruskin was born in London in 1819, and brought up in
rigorously puritanical conditions by his Scottish parents, who
forbade him toys, cake and childhood friends, among other
things. The only relief from the oppressive educational and
religious circumstances of his early life was the occasional tour
the family made in England and abroad (always for business;
never for pleasure), and these clearly had a profound influence
on the observant and sensitive boy. 'The first thing which I
remember as an event in life', he wrote later, 'was being taken
by my nurse to the brow of Friar's Crag on Derwentwater.'

After studying Arts at Oxford, he became a critic of art and
architecture, and in particular made himself the champion of
Turner's painting, which was then startlingly original and
controversial. When he was twenty-eight, Ruskin, still under
the heavy influence of his parents, married Euphemia Gray, a
Scottish girl to whom he was distantly related, and whom he
had known since childhood. But his upbringing had hardly
fitted him for the realities of married life, and after six years the
unhappy Effie ran into the welcoming arms of the painter
Millais.

Ruskin soon became the most famous author of his time in
England, and his writings on matters of art, on which he was
regarded as the greatest authority, expanded into revolutionary socialist theories of morality and economics. He actually
induced Oscar Wilde, among other unlikely navvies, to help
him build a road between the villages of Lower and Upper

Hinksey, near Oxford, to demonstrate the nobility of labour. It ended in a swamp, half finished and very unserviceable!

In 1871 Ruskin bought Brantwood, a dilapidated house on the east bank of Coniston Water. He paid £1500 without even seeing it, because he knew and loved the area and, after much repair and alteration, he moved into the house in the following year, bringing with him his cousin, Joan Agnew, and her husband Arthur Severn, who cared for him in his last years and inherited the house.

Ruskin lived at Brantwood for twenty-seven years, and died there in 1900, after repeated attacks of manic-depression which had been beneath the surface of his highly-strung nature since his youth – 'the dragon that lurks in the bush below', as Burne-Jones called it. Ruskin had gone so far out of his mind that his lectures as Slade Professor of Fine Arts at Oxford were in praise not of Michelangelo or Leonardo, nor even of Turner or Vermeer, but rather of Kate Greenaway.

For the last eleven years of his life, he had been mostly silent, unable to write, or recognize the visitors who came to pay their respects to the prophet he had become, and he would sit for many hours on the stone seat in the grounds of the house. He was buried in the churchyard at Coniston.

Although many of Ruskin's opinions have gone out of fashion, he remains one of the supreme stylists of English literature. His eloquent prose gives him a place among the immortals, even if his views no longer command the reverence that drew such men as Tolstoy and Gandhi to his cause. 'No other man that I met', said Thomas Carlyle, 'has in him the divine rage against iniquity, falsehood and baseness that Ruskin has.'

The bearded patriarch himself was well aware of his failure: 'All my life I have been talking to the people, and they have listened, not to what I say, but to how I say it: they have cared not for the matter, but only for the manner of my words.'

Ruskin's life has become part of the legend of the Lake

The cross over Ruskin's grave at Coniston.

District, and it is perhaps useful to our present purpose, as well as respectful to his memory, to get out of the car and walk in his familiar territory, bearing in mind one of his more enduring aphorisms: 'All travelling becomes dull in exact proportion to its rapidity.'

THE WALK:	MAP SQUARE: E4
CONISTON TO BRANTWOOD	National Grid Ref: SD 303976
	About 6 miles. Easy.

Park in Coniston village, and after seeing Ruskin's grave in the churchyard and visiting the Ruskin Museum if you wish, walk along the main road to the lakeside and round its head, where there are good views of the lake, following the hilly road round the opposite side. Just before you reach a T-junction, take the footpath right, through a gate to the left of a stone barn, and follow this until it rejoins the road, then continue half a mile along the road to Brantwood. The house is now an Adult Education Centre, but it can be visited, and refreshments are available. Ruskin's boat 'Jumping Jenny' is still kept there, and in the garden is the chair made of stone slabs where he used to sit. Return by the same route, enjoying the views of the other *Coniston Old Man across the lake, on which Donald Campbell was killed in 1967 whilst attempting to beat his own world water speed record of 260.35 miles an hour. Coniston Water is certainly a lake of contrasts.*

DEVOKE WATER
AND WAST WATER

Wonderful Walker

The Imperial Heritage

The Tall Story Teller

Many a remarkable tale has been told under the sweeping heading of English 'eccentricity', but for a monumental example of austere living and self-denial during a long lifetime, that of 'Wonderful Walker' surely takes some beating.

Robert Walker was born in the tiny Duddon Valley village of Seathwaite, early in the eighteenth century. He was one of a family of twelve, and was so weak in his infancy that his parents almost despaired of his survival, but they saved a penny or two each week to pay for his lessons in reading and writing, at the school held in the village church.

Eventually, Robert Walker became a teacher himself, at Loweswater. With the assistance of a local gentleman, meanwhile, he himself continued to learn, too, becoming proficient in Latin and Greek. His income was so small that he was forced to keep accurate accounts of even the most trivial purchases, and adding up his expenditure at the end of the year, he was so surprised at the large amount of money he had disposed of that, as Wordsworth put it, 'from that time the rule of his life was to be economical and avaricious'.

Meanwhile, he took holy orders and returned to his birthplace as its curate, at a stipend of five pounds a year. He married a local maidservant, who bore him eight children, and he taught them all himself, in between his other activities.

Besides preaching on Sundays and attending to the wellbeing of his parishioners during the week, he taught the other village children, sheared his own sheep and helped neighbouring farmers shear theirs, as well as helping at lambing time, kept bees to make his own honey, spun and wove his own wool, helping his wife to make clothes for the whole family, tanned the hides of his own cattle, walking to Ambleside – whatever the weather – to sell his produce at the market, nursed his neighbours when they were ill (making them medicines from his own herb garden), helping the local farmers again at harvest time, cutting his own wood for fuel, writing his parishioners' letters for them when they were illiterate (as most of them were and, over the years, seeing his stipend as village curate gradually reach seventeen pounds a year. For a hobby, you might say, he brewed his own beer and sold it, sometimes to his parishioners on Sunday afternoons.

'Wonderful' Walker's church at Seathwaite.

Rev. Walker remained curate of Seathwaite for sixty-six years, and when he died, over ninety years old, he left a fortune for those days of two thousand pounds. The parish register, recording his burial, adds: 'He was a man singular for his temperance, industry and integrity.' Amen to that.

THE WALK:
AROUND SEATHWAITE

MAP SQUARE: D5
National Grid Ref: SD 214954
About 3 miles. Easy.

Drive up the road towards Seathwaite from Ulpha, until you cross the river and arrive at a junction where there is a public telephone box. Park there and walk along the road signposted Seathwaite until you come to the village, passing the inn, and the school where Wonderful Walker taught, and then coming to the little church on the right, where there is a brass plate to his memory, as well as his grave in the churchyard. Cross the road and go over a stile along the side of a field and cross the stream by the footbridge. Follow the path round to the left, and then right again, into a wood, where you soon come to an arched footbridge across the River Duddon. Bearing left, the path brings you into sight of Low Crag on your right. Leave the wood by a kissing gate, and follow the path to a wall, walking along it until you reach a stile. This leads you into a farmyard which you cross and leave by the gate, passing buildings on the left and leading to a track between two walls. The path becomes a hard lane as it approaches the river. Keep on it alongside the river for some way until you come to the bridge you crossed in your car, and turning left over this, you are back at your parking place.

11. THE IMPERIAL HERITAGE

In the dark days of prehistory before the Romans conquered this island, the north of England was occupied by a warlike Celtic tribe known as the Brigantes. It seems unlikely that there was anything more than very scattered settlement in the unhospitable mountain region, and as the Roman legions moved northward under the governorship of Agricola, they cannot have regarded the inhabitants of the Lake District as much of a threat. By AD 81 Agricola had extended the Roman empire as far as the Forth–Clyde isthmus, where the Antonine Wall was subsequently built. The red-haired Caledonian barbarians to the north were by then of little interest to imperial ambitions.

Before Agricola was recalled to Rome, however, his military target had been to conquer the whole island. Rebellious northern Britons constantly sought the aid of their Scots neighbours in raiding Roman positions, and Roman strategy necessarily involved defence against Caledonian attacks by sea as well as by land. It was probably for this reason that Agricola decided to establish a port on the north-west coast at what is now Ravenglass. He may also have planned to launch an invasion of Ireland from it.

With that engineering audacity that typifies Roman imperialism, Agricola linked Ravenglass with the inland military networks by building a road straight across the mountains to the coast from the civil settlement at the head of Windermere – now Ambleside. At each end, and half-way along it at one of its highest points, he built forts to protect it. The one now known as Hardknott Fort, standing on a triangular plateau, had granaries, baths and a parade ground, in addition to the centrally heated quarters, and a gate in each of its four stone walls. It occupies a spectacular site overlooking Eskdale, with dramatic drops on two sides, but the troops who were posted here must have been among the loneliest soldiers in the whole empire, and they were probably under little threat. Five hundred men may have been stationed in this remote stronghold at one time. Agricola perhaps over-estimated the ambition and organizing ability of the Celtic enemies of Rome.

The isolated mountain fortress has been plundered for its building stone over the centuries. It is said that local farmers carried stone away by the cartload in the nineteenth century. Some of the walls have since been rebuilt by the Ministry of Works, to preserve the layout and prevent further ruin, but the remains of the fort still attest to that military and engineering genius which, nearly two thousand years ago, made the Roman Empire the great human adventure that it was.

The Roman fort at Hardknott, with Eskdale beyond.

*Hard Knott Pass is the most difficult motor road in England.
Nearly 1300 feet up at its peak, it is a tightly bending road with
one-in-three gradients, and is certainly not for nervous drivers or
temperamental vehicles. However, you can reach the fort from the
western side by parking near the foot of the pass, just after crossing
the cattle grid, and walking up to the ruins. Those who drive up
from this direction can continue over Wrynose Pass towards
Ambleside, or turn right at the other side of Hardknott towards
Broughton in Furness. There are parking areas beside the road near
the fort.*

*You can wander round the remains at will, and reflect on what
manner of men they were who, bronzed by their native Italian
sunshine, built and manned an outpost of empire in such a wild
and dramatic setting, spending their winters here in one of the
wettest and windiest parts of England, far away from home.*

12. THE TALL STORY TELLER

They used to boast at Wasdale Head that they had Lakeland's highest mountain, its deepest lake, its smallest church and its biggest liar. They were wrong about the church, but they could lay indisputable claim to Scafell Pike, Wast Water and Auld Will Ritson.

The men of Cumbria have long been famed for telling tall stories, and all of them are ready to acknowledge the superiority, in this respect, of the former landlord of the Wasdale Head Inn. Will Ritson was born three years after the Battle of Trafalgar, and died in 1890. Visitors came from far and wide to hear this famous jester telling a tale in his broad dialect, as he held court in his little back kitchen, sitting on a wooden bench. An inveterate foe of urban airs and graces, he was as indifferent to the social standing of his visitors as he was impervious to the influence of cultivated accents.

Once, noting the sensitivity of a group of women he was talking to, he embarked on a sad account of a family of eight – father, mother and their six children – who had been caught in a cloudburst when they were walking on the local fells. In their alarm and anxiety to get home, they had unknowingly waded right into the raging water and, unable to help each other, all eight had lost their lives when they were swept away.

The women were lost for words, silenced by this awful tragedy. 'Ah weel,' said Will Ritson, after a suitable pause, 'it might ha' beean worse!' The women looked at him dumb-founded. 'Worse?' one of them gasped. 'Aye,' said Will, 'it might ha' beean true.'

Will might solemnly explain to a gullible guest how he had once crossed a dog with an eagle, the better to get his sheep off the fells; or how he had once grown a turnip so colossal that a young bullock had got lost eating his way into it. On one occasion he persuaded some anglers that they were failing to get bites because the trout were 't'other side o't'tarn', and sent some of them trekking round to beat the water with sticks to frighten the fish across to their waiting friends.

In an area where tall stories were told with such expertise that they became part of the folklore, a man as famed as Will had to be good. He had to compete with stories like the one about building a wall all round Borrowdale to prevent the cuckoo from migrating, so that it would always be springtime there. Alas, the wall proved not to be high enough, but as the bird flew over it, one of the dalesmen said: 'By gow, if we'd nobbut laid another line o' stanes atop, we'd a copped 'im!' (I think this story is an embroidered version of a tale told of the Wise Men of Gotham, but that is by the way.)

When a competition was organized to find out who could tell the biggest lie, Will Ritson won it with one sentence. After the other competitors had recounted their sometimes laborious and always incredible tales, amid gaiety and laughter, it came at last to Auld Will's turn. To the astonishment of the expectant audience, the famous story-teller said he wanted to withdraw from the competition. Could Will really be throwing in the towel so easily, they wondered. They asked him why.

'Because I cannot tell a lie,' said Will. They awarded him the championship without further ado.

THE WALK:	MAP SQUARE: C3
ROUND WASDALE HEAD	National Grid Ref: NY 187085
	An easy walk of 2 miles.

There is only one road to the village of Wasdale Head, but as it skirts the length of Wast Water, it is a most interesting route. Leave the A595 at Gosforth (not far from Windscale and the Calder Hall Nuclear Power Station) and follow the road through Nether Wasdale, bringing you to the lakeside. Then drive along to the northern end of the Lake. Wast Water is a dramatic and unique sight. The dark screes on the far side drop almost vertically into the water and are reflected in the black depths, while beyond are the slopes of Scafell. Drive on for three-quarters of a mile past the end of the lake, crossing Mosedale Beck by Down-in-the-Dale Bridge, and round the next left bend you reach an open green area where you can park.

Great Gable from Wasdale Head.

Walk back down the road until you have crossed the bridge again and turn right over the stile along the path following the beck. Eventually you cross two more little becks and then come to a packhorse bridge over the main stream, beyond the white inn building. Turn left after crossing the bridge into the village, and follow the opposite bank left, crossing another beck until you see a path following yet another stream to the right, with a wall on the right. Crossing this stream by a little wooden bridge, you can now see the gap between Great Gable and Scafell leading to Styhead. I hope you have a fine day for your walk, for no tall stories are necessary to emphasize the variety of Lake District weather. Through the aforesaid gap are Styhead Tarn and Sprinkling

Tarn, which are in The Guinness Book of Records *sharing the doubtful honour of being the wettest places in England.*

Follow the track as it crosses the beck twice more until you reach a gate, and go through this to the farm at Burnthwaite, walking through the farmyard and over the cattle grid right. The path is then clear past Wasdale Head church and back to your car. The church, though not actually the tiniest in England, is certainly quaint. The roof beams are said to be from ships wrecked on the coast, and buried in the churchyard are victims of mountaineering accidents. There is a Mountain Rescue Post here, and a public telephone box stands outside the hotel.

BUTTERMERE AND CRUMMOCK WATER
The Buttermere Beauty

13. THE BUTTERMERE BEAUTY

Mary Robinson, whose father kept the inn called 'The Char' at Buttermere (now the Fish Hotel) was, by general consent, a real peach. Because she helped her father by serving customers at the inn, her reputation soon spread beyond the locality, aided by a reference to her in a book by one Joseph Palmer, who visited the inn in 1792. And if the title of this true story sounds like some rare species of butterfly, that is not inappropriate, for its subject fluttered unwittingly into the nation's consciousness and was pinned like a collector's specimen in a glass case.

'She brought in part of our dinner,' Joseph Palmer wrote, 'and seemed about fifteen. Her hair was thick and long, of a dark brown, and though unadorned with ringlets, did not seem to want them. Her face was a fine oval, with full eyes and lips red as vermilion. Her cheeks had more of the lily than the rose . . .' Palmer added that, seeing her dancing later, he had never seen more graceful dancing or a woman of finer figure to set it off.

Naturally, all the men who heard of Mary Robinson came to inspect this modest and becoming creature, who was soon famous locally as the 'Beauty of Buttermere'. Even Wordsworth, Southey and Coleridge were drawn to the inn to see if the reputation was justified, and Wordsworth later introduced Mary into his great auto-biographical poem 'The Prelude', referring to his admiration of her modest mien and carriage, marked by unexampled grace.

Not surprisingly, with a continuous procession of admirers visiting 'The Char', Mary not only brought her ageing parents much good business, but eventually – when she was about twenty-five – she accepted a proposal of marriage from one of her visitors. Her betrothed was Colonel the

Hon. Alexander Augustus Hope, no less – Member of Parliament for Linlithgow and brother of the Earl of Hopetoun, and the couple were married at Lorton church on 2 October 1802.

Although the simple local people were as much impressed as Mary was by this gentleman's airs and graces, however, certain more worldly Lakeland residents, among whom was Coleridge, were a little suspicious of the Hon. Alexander's lack of deportment and his ungrammatical speech. So much so that the London newspaper *The Sun* got wind of the story through Coleridge. (The delights of page 3 were unheard of in those days. Otherwise what further notoriety might the unfortunate Mary have been exposed to!) The paper made enquiries which revealed that the real Colonel Hope had been abroad all the summer and was living in Vienna. Mary's husband was an impostor! Further investigation proved him to be one John Hatfield, a linen draper's salesman, who already had a wife and family living in Devon. He was well known in the London coffee houses as Lying Hatfield, had spent some time in various prisons, and had recently been declared bankrupt. Thus found out, Hatfield made himself scarce, leaving Mary pregnant. A very precise description of the wanted man was put out, calling him a 'Notorious Impostor, Swindler and Felon'. He was soon arrested by Bow Street Runners near Swansea, and indicted on three charges of forgery.

Mary was not called to give evidence – forgery was a capital charge and the illegal marriage was relatively trivial as far as the law was concerned. She was required only to testify to the magistrate that she had been deceived, which she did in a note:

'The man whom I had the misfortune to marry, and who has ruined me and my parents, always told me

he was the Hon. Colonel Hope, the next brother
of the Earl of Hopetoun.

Your grateful and obedient servant,
Mary Robinson.'

How much pain lay behind that simple statement we can only imagine. Hatfield was found guilty of forgery at Carlisle Assizes and sentenced to death. It is rather sobering today to realize that the sum of money involved in what the judge called 'crimes of such magnitude as have seldom, if ever, received any mitigation of capital punishment', was fifty pounds. It is generally thought that the jury might have been reluctant to find the man guilty if they had not been aware of his cruel deception of Mary Robinson. At any rate, he was hanged from a tree on 3 September 1803.

Needless to say, the notoriety of the case led to hordes of the curious coming to get a glimpse of the famous victim, who continued to work at the inn for some time afterwards. Melodramas about the case were produced on the London stage. It is not known for certain what happened to Mary's child. Wordsworth's reference to a 'nameless babe' is taken to mean that it was stillborn or died before it was christened, but he could simply have meant that it was illegitimate.

Mary herself married again some years later, and lived – apparently happily – as a farmer's wife, out of the public eye, at Caldbeck. She died in 1837, about fifty-eight years old, and was buried in Caldbeck churchyard, where the gravestone of the 'Beauty of Buttermere' can still be seen.

THE WALK:
ROUND BUTTERMERE

MAP SQUARE: C3
National Grid Ref: NY 170175
An easy walk of about 5 miles,
but may be wet underfoot.

The Fish Hotel, Buttermere.

There are parking places and public conveniences in Buttermere village, where you will see the Fish Hotel and the Bridge Hotel close together. (It is worth a short digression here to explain that a 'char', after which the Fish Hotel was named in Mary Robinson's time, is a small trout or salmon caught only in Windermere, and is a delicacy not to be missed if you get the chance to try it.)

Going to the left of the Fish Hotel, follow the track across the meadows to the lakeside. Buttermere is owned by the National Trust, and is especially renowned for its reflections, being set deep among the surrounding fells, and well wooded with conifers. The footpath is easy to follow round to the right or north-west corner of the lake, and here you will cross a stream which rushes into the lake through a series of cataracts, known as Sour Milk Gill. (There is a footbridge, of course – I do not mean that you have to wade through it!) The path then keeps fairly close to the lakeside through Burtness Wood, making a detour through the farm at the head of the lake, then joining the road for a short distance, and back towards Buttermere via a path tunnelled through the rock. (It is said the one-time owner had this cut to give his staff something to do!) The steep slopes of the fells rise on both sides of the lake and are very imposing. You can also take a pleasant half-mile stroll, going right of the Fish Hotel, to the southern end of Crummock Water.

DERWENT WATER
AND THIRLMERE

The Other Lake Poets

The Island Hermit

The Bowder Stone

The Mystery of the Floating Island

A Tale of H_2O

The Bridal of Triermain

It's Nobbut Me!

14. THE OTHER LAKE POETS

The first reference to the 'Lake School' of poets was not made until 1817, by which time Wordsworth, the native, was approaching fifty, Southey had been living at Keswick for fourteen years, and Coleridge's poetic genius had already dried up. Still, the title caught on, as everyone knows, and it is time we took a closer look at Wordsworth's partners in rhyme.

Robert Southey, Wordsworth's junior by four years, was born in Bristol and educated at Westminster School and Oxford, where he first met Samuel Taylor Coleridge, who was two years older. The two men planned to found an idealistic settlement in America called a 'pantisocracy' and, to that end, considered it important to be married. Southey was already engaged to one Edith Fricker, and Coleridge married Edith's sister Sara. The utopian project fell through, however.

Coleridge then formed his intimate association with Wordsworth, as his neighbour at Nether Stowey in Somerset, and here he wrote *The Ancient Mariner* and *Kubla Khan*. In 1800, Coleridge and his family moved to Greta Hall, near Keswick, where his brother-in-law eventually joined him. 'I question if there be a room in England,' Coleridge wrote, 'which commands a view of mountains, and lakes, and woods and vales superior to that in which I am now sitting.' And he wrote enthusiastically to Southey: 'The house is full twice as large as we want; it hath more rooms in it than Alfoxden: you might have a bed-room, parlour, study, etc, etc, and there would always be rooms to spare for your or my visitors. In short, for situation and convenience – and when I mention the name of Wordsworth, for society of men of intellect – I know no place in which you and Edith would find yourselves so well suited.'

Ironically, Southey had not intended to stay at Keswick for long, but remained there for the rest of his life. Coleridge, on the other hand, ill, restless, unhappily married and addicted to opium, soon went off, leaving his family to the care of Southey, and after various brief wanderings, ended up in the house of a surgeon in London, with whom he passed the rest of his shattered days.

Robert Southey was a prolific author who became Poet Laureate when Sir Walter Scott declined the honour in Southey's favour. He is now remembered more for his prose works, such as the classic *Life of Nelson* and *The Doctor*, in which – among other things – he created the fairy story of Goldilocks and the Three Bears. He was an unselfish and hard-working man of fine character, and his grave in Crosthwaite churchyard has been restored by the Brazilian Government, in recognition of his *History of Brazil*. He was a man of strict habits, who once told a lady visitor: 'I rise at five throughout the year; from six till eight I read Spanish; then French, for one hour: Portuguese, next, for half an hour – my watch lying on the table; I give two hours to poetry; I write prose for two hours; I translate so long; I make extracts so long . . .' and so on, throughout the day. He once sent Shelley into a deep sleep by forcing him to listen to a reading of one of his (Southey's) long poems.

Coleridge, on the contrary, was a man of powerful intellect who is known to almost everyone for his wonderful romantic poem *The Ancient Mariner*. But he was, as Charles Lamb said, 'an archangel a little damaged'. Unsettled, frequently depressed, and a born sufferer, his character let down his undoubted genius. It seems he once went in despair to a clergyman friend for advice on what he should do about his wife's intolerable conduct. Trying to ascertain the nature of her behaviour, the clergyman found Coleridge tearful and incoherent, saying only that he could never live with her again if she were not brought to her senses. Satisfied at last that she had committed no moral outrage, the clergyman began to fear that Mrs Coleridge had gone out of her mind, until at last, after much pleading, he persuaded Coleridge to tell him what she had done – that on the coldest winter mornings she made him get up in his night-shirt and light the fire before she would get herself and her child out of bed.

Well, neither Southey nor Coleridge were 'Lake Poets' in the sense that Wordsworth was, for the native blew the very breath of Lakeland life into his finest works, but all three were men of great gifts, and it is natural that their years of friendship and close co-operation should have linked them together in the public mind.

Coleridge died in London in 1834, at the age of sixty-one. Southey outlived him by five years. Wordsworth outlived them both.

Greta Hall, home of Coleridge and Southey.

THE WALK:
AROUND KESWICK

MAP SQUARE: D2
National Grid Ref: NY 266235
Stroll at leisure. Easy.

Keswick is a fine town of stone on the River Greta, near the north-east shores of Derwent Water, with Skiddaw and Saddleback towering above it. It was once a mining town, and is still famous for making lead pencils, but it is now chiefly a tourist centre, ideal for northern Lakeland, and well worthy of exploration for its own sake.

The Fitz Park Museum, on the north side of the river in Station Road, has manuscripts by Wordsworth, Southey, Ruskin and Sir Hugh Walpole. The Royal Oak Hotel can claim Wordsworth, Southey, Coleridge, Sir Walter Scott, Lord Tennyson and Robert Louis Stevenson among its visitors. The grave of Sir Hugh Walpole is in St John's churchyard.

Greta Hall is not open to the public, being part of a girls' boarding school nowadays, but you can see the building, on a slight eminence, by walking west from Main Street, over Greta Bridge towards Crosthwaite, and looking back from the road.

The parish church of St Kentigern is half a mile farther on. Southey is buried in the churchyard, and in the church there is a recumbent effigy of the poet in white marble, with an epitaph by Wordsworth.

15. THE ISLAND HERMIT

Right in the centre of Derwent Water is St Herbert's Island, so named because the saint is supposed to have lived on it in the seventh century. The Venerable Bede tells the story in his Ecclesiastical History and also in *The Life and Miracles of St Cuthbert*, as follows:

'Now there was a venerable priest of the name of Herebert, who had long been united to the man of God, Cuthbert, in the bond of spiritual friendship, and who, leading a solitary life, in an island in the large marsh from which the Derwent rises, used to come to him every year, and receive from him admonitions in the way of eternal life. When this man heard that he was stopping in that city, he came according to his custom, desiring to be kindled up more and more by his wholesome exhortations in aspiring after heavenly things. When these two had drunk deeply of the cup of celestial

Derwent Water. St Herbert's Island is on the left.

wisdom, Cuthbert said, among other things, "Remember, brother Herebert, that you ask me now concerning whatever undertaking you have in hand, and that you speak to me about it now, because, after we shall have separated, we shall see each other no more in this life. I am certain that the time of my death approaches, and the time of leaving my earthly tenement is at hand." Upon hearing these words, he threw himself at his feet with tears and lamentations, saying, "I beseech you by the Lord not to leave me, but be mindful of your companion, and pray the Almighty Goodness that, as we have served Him together on earth, we may at the same time pass to heaven to see His light. For I have always sought to live according to the command of your mouth; and what I have left undone through ignorance or frailty, I have equally taken care to correct, according to your pleasure." The bishop yielded to his prayers, and immediately learnt in spirit, that he had obtained that which he had sought from the Lord. "Arise, my brother," says he, "and do not lament, but rejoice in gladness, for his great mercy has granted us that which we asked of Him." The event confirmed his promise and the truth of the prophecy; for they never met again, but their souls departed from their bodies at one and the same moment of time, and were joined together in a heavenly vision, and translated at the same time by angels to the heavenly kingdom.'

St Cuthbert was the Bishop of Lindisfarne. Bede claimed to have written his life story from the 'unimpeachable testimony of faithful men', and the remains of the hermitage where St Herbert lived on the island were seen by Wordsworth:

'There stood his threshold; there was spread his roof,
   That sheltered him, a self-secluded man,
   After long exercise in social cares,
   And offices humane, intent to adore
   The Deity with undistracted mind,

And meditate on everlasting things
In utter solitude.'

Although we know nothing of St Herbert but what Bede tells us, it is certain that he was revered locally, for his cult was revived in the fourteenth century, and on the anniversary of his death each year, the Vicar of Crosthwaite went across to the island to celebrate mass in the saint's memory, and the Bishop of Carlisle granted forty days' indulgence to all those who attended the service.

THE WALK:	MAP SQUARE: D2
WEST SIDE OF	National Grid Ref: NY 247212
DERWENTWATER	About 2½ miles. Easy.

Leave your car in the car park opposite St Herbert's Island on the Grange-in-Borrowdale road. Walk back along the road to the loop to the left, where a footpath leaves the road on the right. Turn right at the crossing of the paths and then bear right at the next junction, where the path brings you alongside a wall. Follow the path along the edge of a small wood with the lake on your left and Cat Bells above you on the right, crossing one or two small streams. Then into Brandelhow Park by a gate, and through the woodland, crossing more streams and bearing left at the fork. Sir Hugh Walpole lived at Brackenburn by the road a little way to the south, and set his famous Herries Chronicle *in the district. As the path approaches the bank it doubles back and you can walk along the lakeside towards the island, following the path back to the track near the road where, turning left, you return to your starting point.*

16. THE BOWDER STONE

One of the most curious aspects of Lakeland folklore is that no surviving legends have attached themselves like limpets to the famous Bowder Stone, that massive rock that stands miraculously and self-consciously poised near the Jaws of Borrowdale, like an enormous lady standing on tiptoe as if to convince us that she is a prima ballerina. Apart from the possible derivation of its name from Balder, one of the sons of Odin, there is no popular tale to account for it. The guide books say that two people lying down on opposite sides of its resting point can shake hands beneath it. I do not recommend that visitors put this theory to the test, however. Nature is all too unpredictable. One day the Bowder Stone may topple over, and who knows what day that might be?

This extraordinary boulder has been a popular curiosity ever since tourists first set foot in the beautiful Borrowdale, even though they came to it with some trepidation. Thomas Gray, visiting the dale in the autumn of 1769, wrote about a 'turbulent chaos of mountain behind mountain', and heeded the advice of guides in the Swiss Alps, where you were told to 'move with speed, and say nothing, less the agitation of the air should loosen the snows above . . .'

Nevertheless, visitors to Cumbria found the prospect of seeing this strange boulder too compelling not to risk the hazards of Borrowdale, which they soon found to be exaggerated, and speculation on how the stone got there became a favourite pastime.

Southey later satirized the showbiz exploitation of the Bowder Stone, saying that a certain Mr Pocklington, who owned the land on which it stood, had built 'a little mock hermitage, set up a new druidical stone, erected an ugly house for an old woman to live in who is to show the rock, for fear travellers should pass under it without seeing it, cleared away all the fragments round it, and as it rests upon a narrow base, like a ship upon its keel, dug a hold underneath through which the curious may gratify themselves by shaking hands with the old woman'.

The Bowder Stone.

If only the ancient Greeks had ventured this far, can we believe they would not have invested the lakes and this rock with magical properties, and told stories of how the gods put it there, or how Heracles was challenged to move it, whilst Aphrodite, nonchalantly casting off her silver-edged mantle of clouds, gazed vainly at her reflection in seventeen jewelled mirrors?

As it is, the boulder stands there with a ladder at its side, so that you may climb to its thirty-two-foot-high summit and view the surrounding scenery, which consists chiefly of more rock and a National Trust car park; and science, rather than folklore, accounts for its presence there, confidently asserting that it was carried thither from Scotland by the movement of ice during the glaciation period, and with matter-of-fact procedure reckoning its weight at nearly two thousand tons. It seems a pity that the English imagination has not accounted for it in more romantic fashion. Facts, after all, are ten a penny, and romance is a rare commodity these days.

Personally, I think the Bowder Stone might have been put there by the wizard Merlin, with a sword underneath it, and a promise that whoever could withdraw the sword without toppling the stone should marry the lady of the lakes. No one succeeded, alas. The sword lies rusting below the soil, buried eventually by the weight of the rock, to this day, and the beautiful lady remains in her deathless slumber, still waiting for some valiant tourist to claim her hand.

THE WALK:	MAP SQUARE: D3
THE BOWDER STONE AND	National Grid Ref: NY 253175
ROSTHWAITE	About 4 miles. Easy, but may be wet.

This walk, as well as showing you the Bowder Stone, includes some of the loveliest river scenery in England. There is a car park on the B5289 road, half a mile south of Grange, quite near the Bowder Stone. A gravel footpath leads to it, from the parking area, past a small quarry. When you have seen the stone, return to the road, then walk south along it, crossing Rosthwaite Bridge, and entering the village. Turn right in the village centre, opposite the Royal Oak, and follow the lane bearing right until it brings you to the River Derwent. Turn right along the bank and in a little while cross the river by the bridge, turning right to follow the footpath along the opposite bank and, at length, through some woods Leaving the river where it bends to the right, the path passes a camping site, and then leads across open country into Grange village, where there are public conveniences. Turn right and cross the river to rejoin the main road and, turning right on this, walk back to the car park.

17. THE MYSTERY OF THE FLOATING ISLAND

Most guide books will tell you that – apart from one or two diminutive rocks such as Otter Island – Derwent Water has four islands. Sometimes, however, it has five.

In that bay of the lake lying beside Lodore, visitors have been puzzled for centuries by an island which has been argued over, in this locality, as much as the more famous Loch Ness Monster, and for good reason. For sometimes the island is there, and sometimes it is not. What is more, the water of the lake is on occasion subject to disturbances, on perfectly calm and sunny days, and a small boat may be heaved by a sudden swell, caused by what has long been called Derwent Water's 'bottom wind'.

The disappearing island had been noted at least as far back as 1794, when William Hutchinson wrote his *History and Antiquities of the County of Cumberland*, for he, having heard the story but not having seen the island, wrote: 'The tale with which travellers are amused, of a floating island, appears on strict examination to be fabulous.'

Not so. On strict examination, the island is as real as the Bowder Stone not far away, and if you happen to be at Derwent Water towards the end of a long warm spell in late summer, you may be lucky enough to see it. The island appears, on average, about once in every three years. Its measurements vary, but its greatest observed size is said to have been about half an acre.

Jonathan Otley, a clockmaker who became a pioneer student of Lakeland geology, investigated the island in 1814 and analysed it, finding it to be about six feet thick and composed of peat and decaying vegetable matter, with a thin layer of clay soil on top in which plants had rooted. A later investigator, John Postlethwaite, rowed a boat to the island and stepped on to it, after learning that his parents had had a picnic on it. Local Girl Guides have stuck a Union Jack on it and claimed it for England! Landing on the island is not recommended, however. It may look solid enough, but it is unstable and dangerous.

Various explanations have been offered for this natural trick. One theory was that the 'island' was merely the bed of the lake seen when the water-level was particularly low. Another said that 'it was nobbut a floating mass of weeds'. The real secret seems to be that in warm weather the decaying vegetable matter generates so much methane, or marsh gas, that the 'island' becomes buoyant and, detaching itself from the bed of the lake, surfaces – sometimes for only a few days, sometimes for a few weeks. As for the uncanny bottom wind, it remains stubbornly resistant to scientific explanation – if, indeed, it exists at all.

THE WALK:	MAP SQUARE: D2
LODORE FALLS AND	National Grid Ref: NY 267195
ASHNESS BRIDGE	About 3 miles. Part uphill, but
	easy and steady route.

On the B5289 Keswick–Borrowdale road, near the southern end of Derwent Water, leave your car in Kettlewell car park between the road and the shore, near a landing stage. Turn left into the road and walk a few yards until you see an entrance through the wall on the right into the woods. Follow the footpath which turns south through the wood, more or less parallel with the road, crossing two little streams. Soon you come to a wall enclosing the grounds of the Lodore Hotel and, following this, you will hear the waterfall ahead of you. Turn towards the hotel for the best view. Lodore is the third highest waterfall in the Lake District, a magnificent torrent after heavy rain, and made famous by the praise of the lake poets, especially Southey.

After seeing the falls, follow the footpath along the beck uphill to the upper falls and continue until you reach some stone steps which need careful climbing. Keep to the main pathway, going through an opening in a wall and through the wood, and taking the right path at a Y-junction, then the left one at the next. Soon after a sharp right bend through bracken, the path joins a hard track. Follow this to the made-up roadway and, turning left, walk alongside it until the road itself turns towards the lake above precipitous rocks. The scene before you is known, with some justice, as 'Surprise View', and among the surprises may be the floating island, which makes its appearances in the little bay below. You can see Bassenthwaite Lake as well as Derwent Water – the two may have been one great lake thousands of years ago.

The 'Surprise View' of Derwent Water.

Continue along the road until a gateway leads to a bridge and a cattle grid. You then go through another gateway and reach Ashness Bridge beyond a barn on the right. This is one of the best-known views in all Lakeland, with Skiddaw rising beyond Derwent Water. Turn back along the road past the barn and through the gate, then cross a stile you see on the right of a clearing. Follow the path down through the woodland to a stile near

88

the beck, cross this and go left, keeping left when the path divides, until you come to a wall along the roadside. Turn left and go along the path to a gateway, then cross the road and go left until you come back to the car park.

18. A TALE OF H₂O

Before the nineteenth century, tourism – especially in mountainous terrain like that of Cumberland and Westmorland – was not lightly undertaken. A slow and painful process on horseback or on Shank's Gallawa (as they would say here) was only for the most hardy and conscientious sightseer. The Lake District had to wait for Wordsworth and others to sing its praises before larger numbers of people wanted to see it, and modern transport developments eventually made it possible. Hardly had that happened before tourists began to arrive by the coach-load; and sitting quietly at the back of the coach was the Manchester Water Board.

It was, oddly enough, a native of Cumberland who led thirsty Manchester to the water and invited it to drink Thirlmere. John Grave was the son of a saddler in Cockermouth. He went to Manchester as a young man to make his fortune, and was thrice elected Lord Mayor of that city. At the critical moment for the Lake District, Alderman Grave happened to be Chairman of the Corporation's Waterworks Committee.

Manchester originally had designs on Ullswater, because it was larger, and Haweswater, because it was slightly closer to the city, but Grave sold his committee the idea of Thirlmere because it had a lot more rain than the other two, and would cost considerably less to convert into a reservoir and pipe the water 96 miles to Manchester.

There was uproar over the scheme, of course. There have always been those who maintain that absolutely no interference with Nature is justified, even if no one may be left alive to appreciate it. The Bishop of Carlisle deplored the replacement of Nature 'in her most primitive and untouched beauty' by 'engineering contrivance'. Canon Rawnsley, one of the founders of the National Trust, wrote bad propagandist poetry in defence of the lake, and went on about thrushes and squirrels being driven away by this 'inexcusable spoliation'. But the scheme got through Parliament anyway, and in ten years Manchester had bought the lake, dammed the river, raised the water-level by fifty feet, and constructed the longest aqueduct in Britain.

All this happened at the turn of the century, and everyone has got accustomed by now to the fact that Thirlmere is a reservoir. Manchester did its best to please everybody, but that is never possible. New roads were constructed, replacing the difficult old routes round Thirlmere with good carriage-ways and easier gradients, and thousands of trees were planted, but as these were all larch and spruce, many people were antagonized by the prospect of the Lake District being artificially transformed into a coniferous forest. The trees now obscure the views of the lake from the west bank, and it must be said that this was a serious error of judgment. The enlarged Thirlmere is nearly four miles long, and it is the highest of the lakes except for Haweswater.

The Nag's Head Inn at Wythburn, which had been a popular headquarters for climbers of Helvellyn, was demolished by Manchester some years ago, for the inn's effluent disposal threatened the purity of the water supply.

Centrally situated, and flanked on one side by England's third highest mountain, and by rocky crags with tumbling gills on the other, Thirlmere – also variously known at one time or another as Wythburn Lake, Leatheswater and Brackmere – remains an impressive sight, despite almost a century's interference with its natural state. On the east side of the lake's narrow waist, at the foot of the Helvellyn screes, is a rock outcrop called Clark's Lowp ('lowp' being local dialect for 'leap' or 'jump'). It is said that the unfortunate Mr Clark's wife nagged him so much that at last, unable to stand it any longer, he declared his intention to do away with himself and, climbing to the top of this rock, lowped in. One sardonic version of the story says that Clark's wife advised him against hanging or shooting himself, lest he should suffer pain through inefficient execution, and helpfully supervised his leap from the rock into the deepest part of the water.

Subsequently, of course, Manchester acquired Haweswater as well, but that is another story, and by that time, Alderman Grave was in his . . . er . . . final resting place.

Thirlmere.

THE WALK:
WEST BANK OF THIRLMERE

MAP SQUARE: E3
National Grid Ref: NY 318195
Walk as far as you wish. Level and easy.

Despite the heavy cloaking of the lake by woodland, the road along the west bank is more pleasant and dramatic than the busy A591 on the east side. Park in the car park and picnic area on the B5322 near Legburthwaite, below the Castle Rock of Triermain (see next ection). Walk to the end of the lake along the road crossing the 00-foot-high dam, and simply follow the road round. You can see Helvellyn across the reservoir. Clark's Lowp is at the narrow waist of the lake, past the two islands (Deergarth How and Hawes How). If you reach this point and then turn back, the length of the walk is about four miles. The distance right round Thirlmere by road is about ten miles.

19. THE BRIDAL OF TRIERMAIN

A little to the south of Penrith, at Eamont Bridge, with the M6 thundering past nearby, is an ancient circular earthwork eighty-seven feet in diameter, known as Arthur's Round Table. The several associations of Cumbria with that legendary British hero are, to say the least, vague, but in addition to the Round Table, legend has gathered round the so-called Castle Rock, ably assisted by that old romancer Sir Walter Scott.

The 'Castle Rock of Triermain'.

In the middle of the Vale of St John, near a rock formation known as Watson's Dodd, is an outstanding rock, once called Green Crag, which had some resemblance, for imaginative observers, to a castle. Hutchinson, the Cumberland historian, after describing 'various towers, making an awful, rude, and Gothic appearance with its lofty turrets and ruined battlements', went on to warn the visitor against approaching

94

too close, as the castle was supposed to be protected by certain genii' who with 'superior arts and necromancy, will strip it of all its beauties and, by enchantment, transforms its magic walls'.

Sir Walter Scott sprang upon this jot of local superstition and transformed it with equal magic into a tale of Arthurian chivalry, since when Green Crag has been known as the Castle Rock of Triermain.

The long poem tells how King Arthur, riding south from Carlisle after Pentecost, came upon the enchanted castle and found it occupied by fairies, whose queen, Guendolen, entertained him first with a lavish banquet, and then with more personal enticements, persuading the monarch to dally there many days in this joyous company:

> 'Another day, another day,
>   And yet another, glides away!
>   The Saxon stern, the pagan Dane,
>   Maraud on Britain's shores again.
>   Arthur, of Christendom the flower,
>   Lies loitering in a lady's bower.'

When he finally departed to attend to pressing affairs of state, leaving the fairy queen somewhat incongruously pregnant, Arthur pledged his protection to the offspring of their union:

> 'I swear by sceptre and by sword,
>   As belted knight and Britain's lord,
>   That if a boy shall claim my care,
>   That boy is born a kingdom's heir;
>   But if a maiden Fate allows,
>   To choose that maid a fitting spouse,
>   A summer-day in lists shall strive
>   My knights – the bravest knights alive –
>   And he, the best and bravest tried,
>   Shall Arthur's daughter claim for bride.'

More than fifteen years later, at Penrith, a beautiful maiden named Gyneth presented herself to Arthur as his daughter by Guendolen.

As he had promised, the monarch arranged a tournament on the arena, the winner of which should have the honour of marrying Gyneth. Arthur's knights fought valiantly for the hand of Gyneth, but the princess refused to heed her father's wish that none of his men should be allowed to fight to the death, and soon the tournament became a bloody fray. But the wizard Merlin appeared, angered by the needless slaughter, and spirited Gyneth away to the castle where she was born, putting her into a long sleep in punishment for her mischievous influence on the unfortunate Knights of the Round Table.

Gyneth remained in this deep slumber for five hundred years, and none of those who sought her were able to find the enchanted castle, until Sir Roland de Vaux, the Knight of Triermain, who was told the story by a local sage, vowed to have the princess for his wife.

He too, however, failed to find the castle, in spite of many vigils, seeing only the granite rocks, until one night, after terrible storms and unearthly upheavals, he glimpsed the towers and battlements, and when they threatened to dissolve again, hurled his battle-axe at the rocks. This blow revealed a winding stone staircase leading up to the castle gate, on which was a notice warning the knight to go inside only at his peril, but of course the brave Sir Roland ignored this and – surviving all manner of horrors – was then offered great riches, as well as other temptations, by four maidens (somewhat reminiscent of Macbeth's three witches), which he naturally scorned. His troubles were not over yet, however:

> 'On either side a tiger sprung –
> Against the leftward floe he flung

96

The ready banner, to engage
With tangling folds the brutal rage;
The right-hand monster in mid air
He struck so fiercely and so fair,
Through gullet and through spinal bone
The trenchant blade had sheerly gone.
His grisly brethren ramp'd and yell'd,
But the slight leash their range withheld,
Whilst, 'twixt their ranks, the dangerous road
Firmly, though swift, the champion strode.'

At length, passing through assorted vaults and halls, he came
to a bower where Arthur's daughter still slept in her ivory
chair:

'Still her dark locks dishevelled low
From net of pearl o'er breast of snow;
And so fair the slumberer seems,
That De Vaux impeached his dreams,
Vapid all and void of might,
Hiding half her charms from sight.
Motionless a while he stands,
Folds his arm and clasps his hands,
Trembling in his fitful joy,
Doubtful how he should destroy
The long-enduring spell.'

On being gently kissed, the princess awoke, to be carried away
to a blissful marriage by her heroic rescuer amid thunder and
lightning. And though some men claim to have glimpsed the
Castle through the mist now and then, no one since Sir Roland
de Vaux has ever entered it. His tomb is in the chancel of
Lanercost Priory church, for it was his family who founded the
priory.

THE WALK:
THE CASTLE ROCK
OF TRIERMAIN

MAP SQUARE: E2
National Grid Ref: NY 318196
Short stroll at will, or longer
walk if combined with previous
or next section.

You can drive to the foot of the Castle Rock and park there. From Keswick, drive east on the A66 and turn right at Threlkeld on to the B5322. Drive through the Vale of St John until the valley narrows and you come to a Y-fork, then the car park and picnic area, with public conveniences, will be seen just ahead on the right. The Castle Rock is above you. From the Windermere direction, take the A591 along the eastern side of Thirlmere, past Helvellyn, until you come to the junction with the aforesaid B-road near the northern end of the lake. The car park is then a little way ahead on the left.

You need a vivid imagination to see a Gothic castle here nowadays, either from a distance or close at hand. It is a little over half a mile along the road, past a camping site, to the north end of Thirlmere. There is a public telephone box near the junction of the A591 and B5322.

20. IT'S NOBBUT ME!

Everybody's reaction to the term 'Lake Poets' is to think immediately of Wordsworth, Southey and Coleridge, but of this famous trio, only Wordsworth was a native Cumbrian, and it is arguable that John Richardson has a better claim to the title 'Lake Poet' than any of the three of them.

He was born at St John's-in-the-Vale in 1817, the son of a waller (one who builds walls – you cannot call him a bricklayer in this district!). John followed his father in the trade, and when he was a builder in his own right, he restored the church, built the village school and the parsonage, as well as several local houses, and married Grace Birkett of Wythburn, who bore him ten children.

After twenty-five years in the building trade, John decided that he wanted a change, and he became a schoolmaster, teaching the village children in the school he had built himself, next to the church. He died in 1886 after a stroke,

The church of St John's-in-the-Vale.

and was buried in the churchyard, mourned by a great many people who knew John as a modest, sympathetic and kind-hearted man, and admired his work, not only in walling and teaching, but also as a poet in the local dialect.

John Richardson had written poetry all his life, but it was only in later years that he worked at it enough to justify publication. His finest work was undoubtedly the poem which follows – a rare achievement in successfully conveying a tender romance in the gritty Cumberland speech. It is said to be the story of John's own courtship of Grace, narrated by the female partner:

'Ya winter neet, I mind it weel,
  Oor lads 'ed been at t'fell,
An', bein' tir't, went seun to bed,
  An' I sat be mesel.
I hard a jike on t'window pane,
  An' deftly went to see:
Bit when I ax't, "Who's jiken theer?"
  Says t'chap, "It's nobbut me."

"Who's *me*?" says I. "What want ye here?
  Oor fwok ur aw i'bed" –
"I dunnet want your fwok at aw,
  It's *thee* I want," he sed.
"What cant'e want wi' me," says I;
  "An' who the deuce cann't be?
Just tell me who it is," an' then' –
  Says he, "It's nobbut me."

"I want a sweetheart, an' I thowt
  Thoo mebby wad an' aw;
I'd been a bit down t'deal to-neet,
  An' thowt 'at I wad caw;
What, cant'e like me, dus t'e think?
  I think I wad like thee" –

"I dunnet know who 'tis," says I,
   Says he, "It's nobbut me."

We pestit on a canny while,
   I thowt his voice I knet;
An' than I steal quite whisht away,
   An' oot at t'dooer I went.
I creapp, an' gat 'im be t'cwoat laps,
   'Twas dark, he cuddent see;
He startit roond, an' said, "Who's that?"
   Says I, "It's nobbut me."

An' menny a time he com agean,
   An' menny a time I went,
An' sed, "Who's that 'at's jiken theer?"
   When gaily weel I kent:
An' mainly what t'seamm answer com,
   Fra back o't'laylick tree;
He sed, "I think thoo knows who't is:
   Thoo knows it's nobbut me."

It's twenty year an' mair sen than,
   An' ups an' doons we've hed;
An' six fine bairns hev blest us beath,
   Sen Jim an' me war wed.
An' menny a time I've known 'im steal,
   When I'd yan on me knee,
To mak me start, an' than wad laugh –
   Ha! Ha! "It's nobbut me."'

THE WALK:	MAP SQUARE: D2
CASTLERIGG STONE CIRCLE	National Grid Ref: NY 291237
AND ST JOHN'S-IN-THE-VALE	4 miles or 8½ miles. Easy, but
CHURCH	wet in places.

*Drive a little way out of Keswick on the Penrith road, and turn
right on to the road signed 'CASTLERIGG STONE CIRCLE'.*

You come to this prehistoric site very soon and can park there. The 3000-year-old circle of standing stones is in the care of the National Trust. Standing on high ground, the site commands impressive views all round. Return to the lane and, turning right, walk along it to a gate on the right. Through this, a path goes past the fence round the field containing the stone circle, and on over the fields, crossing two dry-stone walls and passing a small wood on your left. Go alongside the wall on your left until you pass through a farmyard, then bear left through a gate and walk on to the main road, turning left there. A few yards along the road is a stile, signposted to ST JOHN'S CHURCH. Cross the field and the stile at the other side, and follow the path through the gates and over the becks, zig-zagging a little until you see a track leading left to a farm. Avoid this, keeping right, and carry on until you reach a hard track which leads you on to the little church of St John's-in-the-Vale and its neighbours.

If you are doing the shorter walk, cross the stone stile opposite the church and go over the stream. Make for the point ahead of you where a wall slopes into a dip, but take care to avoid boggy ground by walking as far round it as necessary. Go over the wall by the stile and then through the dip towards a tarn below. This is called Tewet Tarn. Pass to the right of it and keep on over a stile and through a gate until you come to a track bringing you to a road. Turn left and you are soon at the main road which leads back to the Castlerigg Stone Circle. Turn left off this road, following the sign to the circle, and cross the beck by Naddle Bridge, then go through a gate and cross two fields by gates in the walls, making straight for the farm ahead. This avoids a stretch of the main road, but brings you back to it not many yards from the circle, round a bend left.

For those wishing to make the longer walk, continue along the road past St John's Church, following the main track left and then the minor track right until you come to St John's Beck. Turn right and follow the stream for a while then, after going through a gate, follow the path away from the beck towards another gate. From this point the Castle Rock of Triermain is in view ahead, and you can follow the path until it reaches the river again, then follow it along the valley to the road bridge. Do not cross this (unless you want a closer look at Castle Rock), but go back along the path for about half a mile until the river on your right turns in towards the path again, then past the bridge and towards the river bank until you reach Sosgill Bridge, leading to the main road on the other bank. Do not cross the bridge, but go through a gate on the left, then turn right across a field and cross the stream by a footbridge. Follow the path through a gate and alongside a wall to a grass path which climbs to a little waterfall. A gate takes you on to a path leading past Rake How on your right – an old farmhouse with sycamore trees and yews nearby. Soon you come to the hard road leading to St John's Church left. Return by the same route as the short walk described above.

BASSENTHWAITE LAKE
The Phantom Regiment
The Little People

21. THE PHANTOM REGIMENT

East of Skiddaw and Saddleback is a mountain called Souther Fell (pronounced Souter), of which a strange ghost story is told; not about the spirit of some long-dead local character who haunts the place; nor that of any single unknown ghost; but the apparition of an entire army of cavalry on the march.

The first recorded witness of this phenomenon seems to have been Daniel Stricket, the servant of William Lancaster, who in the midsummer of 1735 observed an army marching on the east side of the mountain near the summit, for over an hour.

Two years later, Lancaster himself saw the army one midsummer evening – half a mile long and marching in ranks of five, and he was subsequently able to show the apparition to members of his family and others, who related before a magistrate what they had seen. Afterwards, some observers were so convinced by what they saw that they climbed the fell to seek traces of hoof-marks, though they found none.

Sceptics dismiss the story as an optical illusion caused by some unexplained atmospheric phenomenon – a possibility that was well known to Shakespeare:

> 'Sometime we see a cloud that's dragonish;
> A vapor sometime like a bear or lion,
> A tower'd citadel, a pendent rock,
> A forked mountain, or blue promontory
> With trees upon't, that nod unto the world,
> And mock our eyes with air.'

I hope, however, that no one in this supposedly materialistic age, in which practically everyone seems to have seen, described or even photographed some unidentified flying object, will scoff too easily at Mr Lancaster's detailed eighteenth-century account of what he saw:

'. . . he frequently observed that some one of the five would quit rank, and seem to stand in a fronting posture, as if he was observing and regulating the order of their march, or taking account of their numbers, and, after some time, appeared to return full gallop to the station he had left, which they never failed to do as often as they quitted their lines; and the figure that did so was generally one of the middlemost men in the rank.'

Souther Fell, with Saddleback (Blencathra) beyond.

A more interesting interpretation of the phenomenon is that the military host was a presentiment of the Scotch Rebellion, which took place in 1745, shortly after the Ghost Army of Souther Fell was last seen.

> 'Look, how the world's poor people are amazed
>   At apparitions, signs and prodigies,
>   Whereon with fearful eyes they long have gazed,
>   Infusing them with dreadful prophecies.'

THE WALK:	MAP SQUARE: E2
ALONG THE EASTERN FLANK	National Grid Ref: NY 363303
OF SOUTHER FELL	About 6½ miles. Quiet and
	easy. Midsummer Eve
	recommended.

Take the A66 Penrith road out of Keswick, and a mile and a half beyond Threlkeld, at Scales, turn left by the White Horse Inn and park just beyond it on the left. Go through the gate on to the narrow surfaced and gated road round the fell side until you reach the house called Souther Fell on the left. Turn right through a gate and follow the gated path down, crossing a beck, until it reaches a road. Turn left on this and follow it until you reach the village of Mungrisdale. Turn back along the narrow lane crossing the river by the bridge near the Mill Inn. The river is the Glenderamackin. Follow the lane through various gates and a farm, with the long ridge of Souther Fell above you on the right, and lovely views of the more distant fells ahead. This very pleasant lane eventually brings you back to your car near the White Horse Inn.

22. THE LITTLE PEOPLE

No book about an area so deeply influenced by the Norsemen would be complete without reference to the little folk who became established in local lore – the elves, fairies, pixies, dwarfs and goblins who inhabited the secret places and the twilight shadows. The people of Lakeland believed in them without question until the present materialistic age drove the forest spirits out of mind. And it seems there are some who do still believe.

One of the most famous stories about them concerns the so-called Millom Hob. Hob is the local version of the European 'kobold' – an imp who is happy in man's company and performs useful services – provided you don't upset him. Millom Castle had a hob, sometimes known as Throb-Thrush, who would do all manner of helpful things as long as he was given a quart of milk porridge as his reward. All the servant girls had to do when they were faced with an unpleasant task was to say, 'I wish Throb would do that', and in the morning they were certain to find the job done.

One day one of the tenant farmers, alarmed at the prospect of a downpour next day, wished that he had his grain housed, and sure enough, when he got up in the morning, the hob had got every sheaf under cover. Unfortunately, however, the weather was unexpectedly fine, and the farmer wished he had left his corn out in the fields. 'Drat that hob!' he said, 'I wish he was in t'millpond.' An ill-advised remark, for next morning he found that all his corn had been dumped in the millpond and ruined.

Castle How, near Bassenthwaite Lake, is a wooded hill with some traces of an ancient fort, and it was not so long ago when some children, playing there with spades, found a little hut with a slate roof. When they returned after lunch, their spades were still there, but the hut had disappeared. They told their ther about it, and a day or two later he went to the hill with his dog and saw two tiny men dressed in green. The dog made for them at once, but some strange force prevented it from reaching them and, as the dog returned to its master, the little green men disappeared.

At the north-west end of Ullswater, on Soulby Fell, there are traces of another fort called Caerthanock, sometimes known as Maiden Castle, and here it is said that a British king built a tower to protect his daughter, whose death by drowning had been forecast by a wicked fairy. The princess grew up in the safety of the castle until she fell in love and planned to run away with her lover, but when she tried to escape through a window, she fell into a water-butt and was drowned.

If you do not believe any of these stories, perhaps I should tell you that an ancient document recording deaths in the parish of Lamplugh, in the seventeenth century, says that three people were 'frightened to death by fairies', and another was 'led into a horse-pond by a will o' the wisp'.

Bassenthwaite Lake.

THE WALK:
CASTLE HOW AND THE FOOT
OF BASSENTHWAITE LAKE

MAP SQUARE: D1
National Grid Ref: NY 199308
About 1½ miles. Easy.

Castle How is above you in the semicircle between the by-road and lake. On the A66 from Keswick, bear left on the Wythop Mill road then park in the by-road near the Pheasant Inn at the junction. Castle How is above you in the semi-circle between the by-road and the trunk road – not an especially secluded spot for the fairies today alas. Beyond the lay-by is an open gateway on the left through which are a few stone steps leading to an overgrown footpath over Castle How. It is only a few minutes' walk over the top and down the other side.

Having seen Castle How, walk back along the by-road, keeping right, and cross (carefully) over the A66 at the crossroads. The road crosses a beck and then comes to a Y-junction. Keep right, then go left along a footpath, opposite the Bassenthwaite Sailing Club, across a field, which brings you on to a lane. The high ground to your left front is Elva Hill – another indication of the influence of the little people hereabouts. There is a stone circle on its southern slopes. When the lane reaches the road junction, turn right and walk along the road to the bridge, where the Derwent begins its journey from the lake to the sea. Do not cross the bridge, but keep right and walk along the lakeside until you come back to the main road and, crossing this again, you reach your parking spot.

ULLSWATER AND HAWESWATER
Emma and Sir Eglamore
The Village beneath the Lake

23. EMMA AND SIR EGLAMORE

Near the west bank of Ullswater, the second largest of the lakes, are Gowbarrow Park and Aira Force, both owned by the National Trust. Ullswater has, perhaps, what Wordsworth called 'the happiest combination of beauty and grandeur, which any of the Lakes affords,' and he recommended Gowbarrow Park as one of its best vantage points.

It was near this park, with its herds of deer, where William and Dorothy Wordsworth came across the 'host of golden daffodils' that Dorothy described in her journal and William in his more famous poem. 'When we were in the woods beyond Gowbarrow Park,' Dorothy wrote, 'we saw a few daffodils close to the water-side. We fancied that the lake had floated the seeds ashore, and that the little colony had so sprung up. But as we went along there were more and yet more; and at last, under the boughs of the trees, we saw that there was a long belt of them along the shore, about the breadth of a country turnpike road. I never saw daffodils so beautiful. They grew among the mossy stones about and about them; some rested their heads upon these stones, as on a pillow, for weariness; and the rest tossed and reeled and danced, and seemed as if they verily laughed with the wind, that blew upon them over the lake . . .'

Aira Force tumbles over the rocks into a deep glen full of fern and hawthorn, and it is here where the tragedy of Emma and Sir Eglamore is said to have occurred. It seems that Sir Eglamore had been away so long on a Crusade that his beautiful and beloved Emma became ill, and had taken to walking in her sleep. Returning at last unexpectedly, the knight came upon Emma walking like an apparition on the banks near the falls. Startled by the sight, he watched her absently breaking twigs from the trees and throwing them into the rushing water. Then he approached and touched her

Aira Force.

ently, but she awoke from her sleep so suddenly that she
shrieked with alarm and fell backwards over the rocks. Sir
Eglamore plunged into the water to rescue her, but could not
save her life and, heartbroken, he became a recluse, living in
a hut on the edge of the falls and mourning his intended bride
in lonely sorrow.

Wordsworth's poem 'The Somnambulist' is based on this
legend.

THE WALK:	MAP SQUARE: E2
AIRA FORCE AND	National Grid Ref: NY 401201
GOWBARROW PARK	About 2½ miles. Steep in
	places, but mostly a steady
	climb and descent. Care
	needed, but not strenuous, and
	very rewarding.

Park your car in the Aira Green car park (where there are public
conveniences) near the junction of the A5091 and the Ullswater
lakeside road. Go through the gate at the opposite end of the car
park from the road, and cross the field before you, by the main
footpath. Then follow the path through a kissing gate on the right
into the wood. Cross Aira Beck by the footbridge, bearing right up
rough steps. When you come to a fork, take the left path and then
cross the stone bridge for the best view of the waterfall. The drop is
seventy feet, the fourth highest in the Lake District. Waterfalls are
always seen at their best, of course, after heavy rain, but this also
means that paths will be wet and slippery, and care should be
taken, particularly on slopes.

Follow the pathway round and up more steps until you come to
another bridge, where there is a good view of the falls from above.
Then continue up the path, turning right at the junction and going
down until you reach a left turn where the path goes alongside a
fence for a short distance, then fork left and climb up the hillside.

Here there is a splendid view beyond the head of the lake toward Helvellyn.

Follow the footpath up the slope until you come to a crag (Yew Crag) on the right where there is a fork. There are fine views of Ullswater from the top of the crag. Follow the track right round it, taking special care on the steep descent towards the lake. Bear right into the wood and continue through this to the other side. The path is rough and stony for a while, but soon comes on to level grass and to the edge of another small wood. Ignore the path joining it from the left, and walk along the fence round an open area in which is the ivy-covered Lyulph's Tower. This is an eighteenth-century shooting lodge, but is said to have been built on the site of a castle where Baron L'Ulf once lived, who gave his name to Ullswater. Take the left path at the junction, crossing the beck and returning through the wood to the car park.

24. THE VILLAGE BENEATH THE LAKE

'Haweswater', wrote Wordsworth in his *Guide to the Lakes*, 'is a lesser Ullswater, with this advantage, that it remains undefiled by the intrusion of bad taste.'

Well, that was early in the nineteenth century, before the men from Manchester came prospecting for something more essential than taste. And when Thirlmere no longer supplied sufficient water for the expanding city's needs, the Water Works turned its attention back to Haweswater, which it had always fancied in the first place. This lake, the highest above sea-level in the district, was turned into a reservoir in 1940 with the completion of a 120-foot-high dam costing half a million pounds. It is more obviously a reservoir than Thirlmere, with straight edges and devoid of that scattered life round its banks that lends Thirlmere some pretence of remaining natural, but it is still an impressive sight all the same – wild and remote.

Haweswater had its own proud life once. The road round the west bank passed the farming hamlet of Measand, which actually had its own grammar school, founded in 1711 by Richard Wright for the benefit of the local community. They used to say that the farmers of Measand counted their sheep in Latin. But neither the grammar school nor the road exists now.

At the southern end of the lake was the little community of Mardale, scattered around the church and the Dun Bull Inn. The inn was a community centre, and almost a market place, for the farmers whose Herdwicks and Swaledales grazed the surrounding fells. The postman used to travel twelve miles to the village by bicycle and back from Bampton (and he was rarely late). To save time, he would leave all the mail in a biscuit tin, inserted in a dry-stone wall for the purpose, and blow a referee's whistle to let the villagers know it was there for collection. But the church, the inn and the biscuit tin have all gone now.

The tiny church of Holy Trinity had a little square tower with a golden weathercock on top, and stood in its little churchyard where the graves of the villagers were shaded by yew trees. In 1935, nearly a hundred bodies were dug up and re-buried at Shap. Then the church was blown up, and the farmhouses bulldozed to the ground, as the water gradually rose to ninety-six feet above its former level, and the remains of Mardale were submerged. But some say that the bells of Mardale church can sometimes be heard ringing under the water.

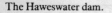

The Haweswater dam.

THE WALK: MAP SQUARE: F3
HEAD OF HAWESWATER National Grid Ref: NY 469108
Short stroll at will. Easy.

*Somewhat tortuous roads lead to Haweswater from Shap or
Askham and along its eastern bank, passing the dam. There are
long-term plans to make this much higher and increase the size of
the reservoir even more. Some of the best views are from the lakeside at this end. About half-way along the lakeside, you pass a
hotel opened in 1937 as the reservoir was being developed, and a
little farther on, beyond the wood, the road crosses two gills. The
second is roughly the point at which the former lake ended.*

*Drive until the road ends at the head of the lake, near a wood,
and park there. The crags of Harter Fell loom up above you.
Walk along the footpath round the lakeside into the wooded
peninsula. At the end of this, looking towards the island, is the site
of the old Dun Bull Inn beneath the water. Continuing round the
edge of the bay to your left, you pass the drowned sites of the little
farming village of Mardale – Chapel Farm and the church, then
Rigaindale Farm and the vicarage. The church stood near the
middle of this little bay, and when the reservoir level is low, after
a long dry spell, you can sometimes see its ruins beneath the water.
Among the crags above you to the right is Eagle Crag, and golden
eagles, which were common here a century ago, have been seen in
the area again in recent years.*

*It is possible to walk right round the lake (distance ten miles),
but the return is on the road you came along, and it is suggested
that you return to your car by the same route when you have seen
enough.*

LAKELAND FRINGES – NORTH

The Lords of Lowther
Long Meg and Her Daughters
D'ye ken John Peel?

25. THE LORDS OF LOWTHER

The gaunt ruins of Lowther Castle, south of Penrith, are among the nearest things we have in England to the spectacular structures of mad Ludwig of Bavaria. They stand roofless and hollow, like an abandoned film set, in their magnificent grounds – haunted, perhaps, by the ghosts of the Viscounts and Earls of Lonsdale who have lived on this estate for many centuries, and entertained on a lavish scale guests such as Mary Queen of Scots and the Emperor of Germany. Yet the castle we see now is not two hundred years old.

Hugh de Lowther was a part-owner of the land here early in the fourteenth century. A hundred years later, his descendant Sir Robert was the sole lord of the manor, and the Lowthers gradually acquired land here and there over the centuries until their wealth and influence rivalled other great northern families like the Percys and the Howards. By the end of the seventeenth century the head of the family was Baron Lowther and Viscount Lonsdale. He was Lord Lieutenant of Westmorland, and had vast farming and coal-mining interests, which included the development of Whitehaven, ironically, as a port for exporting coal to Ireland.

The ancient village of Lowther, which took its name from the river bordering the estate on the west side, was demolished to extend the mansion's grounds. Only the twelfth-century church was left standing, and this was largely rebuilt. The farmworkers and tenants were re-housed in a village called Newtown which was built for the purpose farther east (so as not to block the view), and for a while expensive carpets were made there from the wool of the local sheep. The enterprise was not successful, however, and perhaps with guilty consciences the family began building another estate village, which they named Lowther. This was never completed.

Meanwhile, the park and mansion went on growing. Sir

John Lowther extended the house in the late seventeenth century with stone from Shap Abbey, which he also owned. Wordsworth's grandfather was superintendent of the estate and his father, John Wordsworth, was 'law-agent' to Sir James Lowther, the first earl, who had married the Prime Minister's daughter, and sent nine Members of Parliament to Westminster from the huge territories in his ownership. John Wordsworth was, in reality, his Tory political agent, and when he died, Lord Lonsdale owed him considerable money which he had refused to pay during Wordsworth's lifetime. The poet himself recovered this debt from the second earl, and suddenly found something to admire in the aristocracy after having previously been a left-wing revolutionary!

In the village of Askham.

It was in the early years of the nineteenth century when the last rebuilding of Lowther Castle took place, after the previous mansion had been partly destroyed by fire. The architect was Robert Smirke, who had been recommended to Lord Lowther by that other coal-mining magnate and patron of Wordsworth, Sir George Beaumont. Smirke designed a Gothic fantasy which looked like a medieval castle in one aspect and a cathedral in another. It was the culmination of the growth of Lowther wealth and power, dominating the landscape around it. The main rebuilding of St Michael's church took place some years later, and the curious family mausoleum was built in the churchyard.

Lowther Castle remained the home of the Earls of Lonsdale until 1936, when it was abandoned in favour of the nearby and rather less extravagant Askham Hall. The great mansion was gutted, and it has remained a romantic shell ever since, a symbol of the power that once ruled half of Cumberland.

THE WALK:	MAP SQUARE: F2
ASKHAM AND LOWTHER	National Grid Ref: NY 513237
	About 4 miles. Easy.

Park in the picturesque village of Askham, which is best reached from Penrith or from Pooley Bridge at the north end of Ullswater. Walk east from the village centre, past the church, to the bridge over the River Lowther. Over the bridge, turn right, off the road, up the path through the wood. This soon bends round to the left and leads on to a drive, which brings you into view of the castle ruins. Continue past the fork, to the right, and then take the path to the right, off the drive and parallel with the front of the castle, across the park, until you come to the road at Newtown. Turn right on the road and soon you come to the model village of Lowther.

When you have seen this surprising village, designed by Robert Adam, with uniform cottages of grey limestone in their neat and formal setting, continue along the road to the junction and turn left, then when this road joins the A6, turn left and then left again, off the trunk road almost immediately.

The road you are now on forms the boundary of the Lake District National Park at this point. Go over the crossroads, and follow the road round to the left into the castle grounds again. Keep to the main roadway, ignoring the drives that go off it either side, until you see Lowther's church of St Michael on the right, reached via a wicket gate. The mausoleum will be seen in the churchyard, and monuments to the earlier Lords Lonsdale are in the north and south transepts.

Continue along the road which brings you to the bridge over the river, and back into Askham village.

Part of Lowther Park is a Wild Life and Nature Park, which is well worth a visit, and this is reached from Hackthorpe on the A6 road.

26. LONG MEG AND HER DAUGHTERS

Between Glassonby and Little Salkeld, to the north-east of Penrith, and not far from the River Eden, William Wordsworth one day came upon an ancient stone circle which he knew to be called Long Meg and Her Daughters, and which he described as 'a perfect circle, eighty yards in diameter, and seventy-two in number, and from above three yards high, to less than so many feet: a little way out of it stands Long Meg herself – a single stone eighteen feet high'.

> 'A weight of awe not easy to be borne
> Fell suddenly upon my spirit, cast
> From the dread bosom of the unknown past,
> When first I saw that sisterhood forlorn.'

Other witnesses have described this stone circle differently, however. One book refers to 'an oval setting of fifty-nine stones, each about 10 ft. high, with a maximum diameter of 360 ft'. Another says: '. . . a prehistoric circle . . . composed of 65 stones, exclusive of Long Meg (height 12 feet)'. Never mind her height, one feels inclined to say – how many daughters has she got? Yet another book says: 'Of a former total of 59 stones, 27 are still standing, and perhaps a dozen more have disappeared.'

No doubt all these various authors can count, just as well as you and me, but the plain fact of the matter is that Long Meg and Her Daughters are enchanted, and no one is able to count the stones and get the same result twice. Not only that, but no one knows who placed the stones there, or why. One of the first to describe the circle was Reginald Bainbrigg, an antiquary who wrote, in about 1600: 'Besides Little Salkeld . . . wher the Romaines have fought some great battle, ther standes certaine . . . pyramides of stone, placed ther in the manner of a crown. They are commonlie called meg with hir daughters. They are huge great stones, long meg standes above the ground in sight XV fote long and tre fathome about.'

Long Meg and some of her daughters.

Camden referred to the circle as a Roman monument; Stukeley as a Celtic temple; and more modern writers as a Bronze Age ceremonial circle. Wordsworth opted for the Druid alternative, as befits a poet. What the local folk have known perfectly well for centuries, however, is that Long Meg and Her Daughters were turned to stone for dancing on a Sunday, and if anyone could count them correctly, the spell would be broken.

One landowner sought to put an end to all this nonsense by blasting the stones out of existence, but the workmen he had engaged for the job fled in terror when a frightful thunder-storm threatened to blast *them*, and no one since has tried to remove the petrified sisters by wholesale methods, although a few stones have evidently been broken up and carted away, no doubt to be used as material in some nearby building project.

Personally, I wonder if the popular name for the circle is a corruption from an old and dimly-remembered Celtic folk-tale, 'Longas mac n'Usnig', which tells of the fate of the children of Uisneach. But if you should visit the circle, try counting the stones, and if you get the same number twice, who knows, they may turn into dancing girls before your very eyes.

THE WALK:	MAP SQUARE: G1
LITTLE SALKELD AND	National Grid Ref: NY 566363
LONG MEG	1½ miles. Easy.

Park in Little Salkeld and walk along the Glassonby road out of the village until you come to a crossroads. The road right is signed Hunsonby, but it is the lane to the left you want to take. This shortly brings you to a junction and, turning right, the surfaced lane brings you right to the centre of the circle very soon, with Long Meg herself standing unmistakably to your left, sixty feet south-west of the circle. Return by the same route.

700 yards to the north-east is another, smaller circle of eleven stones known as Little Meg. Some of the stones bear Celtic carvings. This was a burial place, probably of a person of importance, whose cremated remains were buried in an urn.

27. D'YE KEN JOHN PEEL?

The great traditional sports of the Lake District are wrestling and fox-hunting. Wrestling in the dales and hunting on the fells. There was a third – cock-fighting – but that has been illegal since 1835. This was never country where wealthy young bloods in red coats kept stables of horses to gallop in colourful pursuit across the countryside during the day and attend fashionable society balls at night. Here, the fox was hunted on foot, and sensible people who wanted to follow the hunt wore strong boots and whatever clothing would stand up to the weather. There was little glamour or false sentiment about hunting in Cumbria. In country where the economy depended so largely on sheep farming, the fox population had to be kept down. Lakeland sheep were small, and the foxes large. The largest fox recorded in Britain was killed by the Ullswater hunt in 1936. It measured four feet five inches from its nose to the tip of its tail.

The world's most famous huntsman was a Cumbrian farmer. John Peel became a legend in his own lifetime, and his renown has hardly diminished a hundred and twenty-five years after his death. He was born at Caldbeck in 1776, the son of a horse dealer, and he grew up to be a man 'terble lang in t'leg and lish' (active), standing over six feet tall. He was also an individualist from an early age. When he was barely twenty, he asked a local girl of nineteen, Mary White, to marry him. She agreed, and so they went straight to the village rector and asked him to call the banns, which he did on the following Sunday. The congregation was dumbfounded – not least the parents of the couple, who knew nothing of the arrangement. Mary's mother immediately advanced their tender ages as a just impediment, and the marriage was off.

John Peel was not so easily deterred, however. He promptly

saddled his father's best horse and rode the twenty-five miles to Gretna Green with Mary in the saddle behind him, and there they were wed. Afterwards they had a 'proper' marriage in Caldbeck church to please their resigned parents. Mary gave birth to seven sons and six daughters. When her father died, he left to Mary his small estate at Ruthwaite, and here the family lived and managed the farm. Mary lived to be eighty-two, surviving her husband and two of her children.

As a huntsman, John Peel was a fanatic. He would sacrifice everything for the sake of a hunt, and it was said that at one stage he sacrificed the efficient running of the farm, and had to be helped out of financial difficulties by friends and neighbours.

He started his 'career' as huntsman to Sir Frederick Fletcher Vane, of Armathwaite Hall, but soon owned his own pack of twelve couples, and attracted enthusiastic support for his long and exciting hunts, mostly on foot over the fells, but sometimes on horseback, as occasion demanded. Peel was always off at the crack of dawn, in his grey coat woven locally from wool in its natural colour.

Peel's more widespread fame came after his hunting friend John Woodcock Graves wrote the world-famous song about him, one night in 1832, when they were sitting by the fireside together. 'By gok, John,' Graves said, 'thou'll be sung when both of us is run to earth.' And so he was. The words were set to music by the choirmaster of Carlisle Cathedral, and have been sung the world over ever since:

> 'D'ye ken John Peel with his coat so grey,
>   D'ye ken John Peel at the break of day;
>   D'ye ken John Peel when he's far, far away
>   With his hounds and his horn in the morning?'

In his seventies Peel was still hunting, and his last tally-ho came at the start of the season in 1854, when he died on 13 November at the age of seventy-eight. 1854 was the year

IN Memory OF
JOHN PEEL OF
RUTHWAITE. who died
Nov.13th 1854. aged 78 Years.
Also MARY. his wife. who
died Aug.t 9th 1859. aged 82
Also JONATHAN their Son
who died Jan. 21st 1806.
aged 2 Years.
Also PETER their Son. who
died Nov.t 15th 1840.
aged 27 Years.
Also MARY DAVIDSON their
DAUGHTER who died Nov. 30.
1863. aged 48 Years.
Also JOHN their Son who died
Nov.t 22nd 1887 aged 90 Years.

CROSTHWAITE

John Peel's grave at Caldbeck.

134

of the Charge of the Light Brigade on the Russian guns at Balaclava, and it is said that the men of the 34th Foot, subsequently the Border Regiment, whistled the John Peel tune as they helped the cavalry prepare for the attack. The song became the regiment's official march.

It was a more mournful tune that accompanied John Peel's body to his grave in Caldbeck churchyard. As the funeral procession passed the kennels, his pack of hounds set up a howl that was a fitting chorus to this passionate huntsman's last ride.

THE WALK:	MAP SQUARE: E1
CALDBECK AND THE HOWK	National Grid Ref: NY 325397
	A little under a mile. Easy, but
	liable to be wet, and care
	needed in places.

Park in Caldbeck and begin by visiting John Peel's grave in the churchyard of St Kentigern. The elaborate decoration on the headstone to Peel and his family includes a hunting horn.

From the south corner of the large village green, with its duck-pond, go through the big farm gates, where a sign on the wall indicates the way to the Howk. If the big gates are closed, there is a wicket gate you can go through. Go straight ahead over a stile and along the path. Notice ahead of you, before going through a gate, the derelict woollen mill where John Woodcock Graves once worked. Soon the path along the river bank brings you to the limestone gorge known as 'The Howk'. A ruined bobbin mill will be passed in this eerie gorge, where one of the huge swallow holes is known as the Fairies' Kettle, from its appearance when the river is at its most turbulent. We have come across fairies before in this book, and a long cavern nearby is called the Fairy Kirk. Many superstitions are connected with it.

Following the footpath up some steps, cross the beck by the wooden footbridge, and go over the stile into a field. Turn left towards the farm and you will see a stile over the wall. Over this, turn left and walk along the road back into the village. The Caldbeck Fells stretching away to the south were Peel's familiar hunting territory. Fell hunting still goes on there, and copper and lead mining were important local industries on them.

LAKELAND FRINGES – SOUTH

The Bridge Builder from Down Under

The Daughter of Kendal Castle

The Last Wolf

28. THE BRIDGE BUILDER FROM DOWN UNDER

Kirkby Lonsdale is a busy little limestone town tucked between the River Lune and the A65 Lake District road from Yorkshire. Crossing the river, a stone's throw from the main road, is a narrow old three-arched bridge of uncertain origin, built of stone. Some say it was built in medieval times. Some say it was built by the Devil in one night.

It seems there was once an old woman who lived by the banks of the river, and she had a valuable cow, a fine pony and a little dog. One evening, the cow and the pony crossed the river, presumably because the grass is always greener on the other side. But a great storm blew up, the rain poured down, and the river soon swelled to such a torrent that the animals could not get back.

The old woman was in despair. How was she to recover her livestock? At this point, who should put in an appearance but Old Nick himself, and he told the tearful dame not to worry. He would build a bridge across the river by morning, so that she could lead her animals back to safety.

Now of course the old woman was shrewd enough (for she was a Yorkshire woman) to realize that t'owd devil did not propose to do all this work for nowt, so she asked his price, and he slyly told her his only condition – that the first living thing to cross the bridge was to be his. She had no alternative but to agree if she wanted her animals back, but she knew what he was laikin' at, sure enough.

Came the dawn, and she went down to the river bank with her dog, after worrying all night about what was, in those days, a fate worse than death. There stood the bridge as promised – give the Devil his due – and there its infernal builder awaiting her arrival. The old biddy stood on one side of the river and Lucifer on t'other. He politely bade her good morning – for he was a born politician – and invited her to come across to collect her cow and her pony. She stepped forward as if to cross, then drew from the folds of her apron a bun she had concealed there, and threw it across the river to the opposite bank.

Immediately the little dog ran across the bridge to retrieve the bun, and the old woman gleefully pointed out to the Devil that the dog was his by virtue of their bargain. Lucifer was livid! He had quite enough soulless curs already! He vanished in an angry cloud of yellow smoke, and the old woman rounded up cow, pony and dog, and took them all home, across the bridge that remains there to this day.

The Devil's Bridge at Kirkby Lonsdale.

THE WALK:
DEVIL'S BRIDGE AND
KIRKBY LONSDALE

MAP SQUARE: G6
National Grid Ref: SD 615783
1½ miles. Easy – a little care
needed in places.

Park near the River Lune, just off the A65 trunk road, close to the fifteenth-century bridge. Having decided for yourself whether the

Devil or some less impetuous mason built it, walk along the lovely wooded footpath beside the river, in the direction of the town. On our way, you will see some of the huge stones the Devil dropped in his hurry to finish the job in time, and some he left behind when he had finished. From a spot called the Brow, farther along the river past the island, Ruskin called the view of the Lune valley one of the loveliest scenes in England.

Walk up the hill to the left of the unsightly gasholder, looking back for the view of the Pennines and, turning left, go back through the town, with its grey stone buildings and little market square. Turn left when you reach the A65 to get back to your car.

29. THE DAUGHTER OF KENDAL CASTLE

In the old weaving town of Kendal, now better known as the 'gateway to the Lake District', are the ruins of a twelfth century castle. All that remains on the hill, surrounded by a deep (and empty) moat, are some fragments of a circular enclosing wall and three towers, and part of a later range with dungeons below. But the castle's situation is splendid, and it commands fine views of the Lakeland fells.

The powerful family that owned the castle in Tudor times helped to foster the weaving trade which had then grown up in what was called Kirkby Kendal, since Flemish weavers had settled here in the fourteenth century. Coarse Kendal cloth was worn by Londoners and the English soldiers at Flodden Field and, in particular, the colour known as Kendal Green was famous enough to merit a mention by Shakespeare:

> FALSTAFF: As the devil would have it, three misbegotten knaves in Kendal green came at my back and let drive at me; for it was so dark, Hal, that thou couldst not see thy hand.
>
> PRINCE HAL: These lies are like their father that begets them; gross as a mountain, open, palpable. Why, thou clay-brained guts, thou knotty-pated fool, thou whoreson, obscene, greasy tallow-catch, –
>
> FALSTAFF: What, art thou mad? art thou mad? is not the truth the truth?
>
> PRINCE HAL: Why, how couldst thou know these men in Kendal green, when it was so dark thou couldst not see thy hand?

(Henry IV, Part I)

In 1512, at Kendal Castle, a daughter was born to the lord and lady of the manor, and they named her Catherine. Her parents aw to it that she was given a fine education, and she was duly married to Sir Edward Burrough. She was not beautiful. Her portraits show her as a plain young lady, with a Roman nose and thin lips. But she was clearly regarded as a good catch, for – being soon made a widow – she was not long in marrying again, this time becoming the wife of Lord Latymer. Catherine had no children of her own, but brought up three step-children. She had a keen mind, was firmly Protestant in her sympathies, and was something of a blue-stocking, but with a clear sense of duty as a wife and step-mother.

The ruins of Kendal Castle.

When her second husband also died, Catherine, though still young, might have resigned herself to widowhood and pursued her intellectual interests, but two further suitors sought her hand, one of them a fellow named Henry, also married more than once before, who asked her to become his wife and took after him and his children. He was corpulent and ulcerous, but she agreed. Her third husband was fifty-two and his new wife thirty-one. She was Catherine Parr, daughter of Sir Thomas Parr of Kendal Castle. He was Henry VIII, King of Great Britain, France and Ireland, who had had his previous wife's head chopped off in the previous year.

The new queen succeeded beyond all expectation in her role as nurse and step-mother. She drew Henry's three scattered offspring to her, supervised their education and protected their interests with genuine affection. In particular, she was close to Elizabeth, the auburn-haired daughter of Ann Boleyn.

The royal family was not long united, however. Less than four years after the marriage, Henry died, leaving Catherine a widow for the third time, and not yet thirty-five. The new king was Edward, Henry's son by Jane Seymour. Catherine's other suitor, when Henry outbid him for her hand, had been Thomas Seymour, Lord High Admiral and the brother of Henry's third wife. Intent on advancement, Seymour now made a bid for one of the royal princesses – he hardly cared whether it was Elizabeth or Mary – but failing to win either of them, he recovered his interest in the Queen Dowager, and Catherine agreed to marry him.

Seymour was a lecher, whose taste for indecent games included entering Princess Elizabeth's bedroom in the mornings, before she was dressed, and smacking and tickling her. He was also over-familiar with the ladies-in-waiting. Catherine – at first compliant – came to resent her husband's attentions to other women, and no doubt her fourth marriage would also have ended in disaster if she had had to suffer it much longer, but in her thirty-sixth year she became pregnant, and died giving birth to Seymour's daughter.

Thus ended the curiously unfulfilled life of this Westmorland girl, who seemed so full of promise as one of the most cultivated women of the Renaissance. Perhaps her achievement for her country has gone largely unrecognized, however. We cannot tell how much her influence helped to create our greatest queen, who came into her care as a ten-year-old girl, whose own mother had been executed when she was only two, depriving her of a family life and home until the king married Catherine. It was a short-lived union, but perhaps during four of her most formative years, the character of Queen Elizabeth I was moulded more than we realize by the daughter of Kendal Castle.

THE WALK:
AROUND KENDAL

MAP SQUARE: F5
National Grid Ref: SD 517927
Kendal is a place for strolling at leisure rather than organized walking, but the following suggestion covers some interesting ground.

Leave your car at one of the car parks in the town centre, make your way to the main shopping street, Stricklandgate, and walk south, past the Town Hall (Information Centre) into Highgate. Kendal is an interesting old town of wide streets, with grey stone houses and bridges, and many yards and alleys. The Mayor's Parlour contains some paintings by George Romney, best known for his productive liaison (artistically, at any rate) with Lady Hamilton. Also in the Parlour is kept Catharine Parr's tiny 'Book of Devotions', beautifully written in her own hand and bound in silver. Beyond Highgate is Kirkland, where there is a Museum of Lakeland Life and Industry, as well as the parish church of Holy Trinity. This is one of England's largest parish churches, and is unique in possessing four aisles. Walk back along Kirkland and turn right at the crossroads, past the recreation ground, and cross the River Kent by the footbridge. Turn right on the main road (A65) for a short distance, then left into Parr Street. From the end of the street, you can go over a stile straight up to the castle ruins on the circular hilltop. There are fine views in all directions.

Follow the footpath down the castle hill to the left (north) until you reach Castle Road, turning left and then left again into Castle Street. When you reach the crossroads there is, diagonally right, the Castle Dairy, a mainly Tudor building with some fourteenth-century remains, which can be seen for a small entrance fee. Re-cross the river by Stramongate Bridge, continue to Stricklandgate via the market place, and thence to your car.

30. THE LAST WOLF

In a part of England so long dependent for its economy on sheep rearing, it is hardly surprising that many legends are concerned with the wolves that used to roam freely in this country until around the time of Elizabeth I. According to tradition, the last wolf in the Lake District was killed by Sir John Harington, of that old and enterprising family whose members included the inventor of the water closet. (*Lupus* – Latin for wolf: hence perhaps 'loo'?)

The story goes that Sir Edgar Harington, lord of the manor of Wraysholme, near Cartmel, had angrily cut off his son without the proverbial farthing, because he had discovered that John planned to marry his young ward, Adela, without his blessing. John joined a Crusade to the Holy Land and, after some years abroad, returned to Wraysholme unknown to his father. Sir Edgar had just declared that he would give Adela's hand in marriage, as well as half his estates, to any bachelor knight who could slay the wolf which had been marauding in the Cartmel district.

Sir John mounted his valiant steed and set off in pursuit of the lone wolf, which he eventually sighted, and gave chase until he caught up with the exhausted beast on the shore at Humphrey Head, where he killed it, thus winning back his intended bride, his father's love, and his rightful inheritance.

The name Ulpha, from 'wolf', occurs frequently in Lakeland, and in this corner, in particular, survives to the north-east of Grange-over-Sands, not far from the remains of Wraysholme Tower, where the Haringtons had lived since the thirteenth century. One of their number is buried in Cartmel Priory church, beneath a fine fourteenth-century monument, but the fate of the heroic wolf-slayer cannot be traced.

THE WALK:
CARTMEL AND HUMPHREY
HEAD

MAP SQUARE: E6
National Grid Ref: SD 405775
About 8 miles. Uphill for short
distances, but quite easy.

*Drive to Grange-over-Sands, which is well worth a visit for its
own sake, and park your car there. Walk out of the town, away
from the seafront, on the Cartmel road. Go up the hill round the
bend to the left, taking the right turn and then going left across the
golf course round the foot of the fell, rejoining the road nearer
Cartmel. Walk into the attractive village and visit the famous
priory church, where there is a tomb to one of the Haringtons, who
may have been an ancestor of Lady Jane Grey, as well as of the
wolf-slayer.*

An attractive corner in Cartmel.

*Walk along the road south from the church, out of the village
towards Allithwaite, but do not turn left into the village. Go
straight on, downhill and over two crossroads. After a double
bend in the road, you come to the ruins of Wraysholme Tower on*

148

your left, before the railway level crossing. On the other side of the railway, turn left, following the signposted lane to Humphrey Head, bearing right at the junction.

Walk back to the junction and turn right, then at the end of the lane follow a footpath left under the railway and across the field to Allithwaite where, joining the road, you turn right and go up the hill towards Grange-over-Sands, following the main road until, round the left-hand bend, you can leave the main road by turning right towards the sea front and then coming to a path along the front until you come back to the centre of Grange.

LAKELAND FRINGES – EAST
The Terrible Knitters of Dent

31. THE TERRIBLE KNITTERS OF DENT

At the time of the events to be related, the village of Dent was in Yorkshire, and indeed it is still within the Yorkshire Dales National Park, but its strong links with Lakeland would have justified its inclusion in this book, even if the Local Government Act had not recently made a gift of it to Cumbria.

It was Wordsworth who first drew attention to the story by his discovery of an ageing Lakeland character, Betty Yewdale, but it was Southey who made Dent famous.

Wordsworth seems to have met Betty Yewdale at her cottage home at Hacket, not far from Little Langdale. She and her husband Jonathan made a poor living from their smallholding, supplemented by Jonathan's work in one of the local quarries, and Wordsworth apparently encountered Betty outside her cottage one dark night holding up a lantern to light her husband home. Such an image was irresistible to the poet. After talking to her, Wordsworth put the couple into his poem 'The Excursion' as noble peasants of the sort with whom he was wont to romanticize Lakeland:

> 'I never see
> Save when the Sabbath brings it kind release,
> My helpmate's face by light of day. He quits
> His door in darkness, nor till dusk returns.
> And through Heaven's blessing, thus we gain the bread
> For which we pray.'

When Wordsworth had finished drowning the pages of his work in such floods of lofty sentiment, Robert Southey became interested in Jonathan and Betty Yewdale, and after Jonathan's death, when Betty was living at Rydal, Southey's daughter and Wordsworth's sister-in-law went to see Betty on Southey's behalf.

The character who emerged from this interview, and from

subsequent investigations by Dr Alexander Craig Gibson, was rather different from Wordsworth's lonely heroine who patiently tended her plot until her beloved husband came home at the weekend to cheer up their humble home.

'A shrewd and masculine woman was Betty Yewdale,' Southey wrote, 'fond of the nicotine weed, and a short pipe so as to have the full flavour of its essence.' Jonathan, it seems, was a bit simple-minded, or 'short o' leet' as they would say in the neighbourhood. Once, when he had stayed out all night and got drunk after a funeral, Betty descended on the Black Bull at Coniston in a fury, gave Jonathan's companions 'a blackin' as they willn't seeun forgit', and drove her husband home across the fields with a stick, not hesitating to switch him as he crawled through the 'hog-hooals' made in the dry-stone walls for sheep to pass through.

Betty's fame, however, rests in the tale of her childhood she told to Southey's investigators, and which the poet published in his work 'The Doctor'. Betty and her little sister Sally were sent by their father at tender ages to learn a trade. Betty was seven and Sally five or six when they were taken off to Dent to learn hand knitting from the women there who produced knitted garments at such a pace that 'terrible' was the word that impressed itself on young Betty's mind. 'They er terrible knitters e' Dent,' she said.

The two girls did not like Dent at all. 'We went to a skeul about a mile off – there was a Maister an' Mistress – they larnt us our Lessons, yan a piece – an' then we o' knit as hard as we cud drive striving whilk cud knit t'hardest yan again anudder . . . We knit quorse wosset stockings – some gloves – an' some neet caps, an' wastecwoat breests, an' petticwoats.' But all the time the girls' thoughts were on one thing – going home. Whenever they were alone together they planned and talked until, one winter's day, 'we teuk off'.

They set off towards Kendal in the snow wearing only their bedgowns and aprons, clogs and hats, and with sixpence in

Betty's pocket, which they gave to a Scotswoman who took them in for a night and gave them bread and milk.

Eventually, the sisters arrived at Kendal, sodden with rain, where a woman took pity on them, fed them and dried their clothes, and found them a bed in a house where an old woman in the same room had a fit during the night. Next day they pressed on, stopping now and then for a rest, sometimes crying, rubbing each other's hands to warm them, and increasingly anticipating their parents' anger when they got home.

It was two o'clock in the morning when they arrived, and cried out until their mother heard them and got up to let them in, 'as neer deead as macks nea matter . . . they warrant a bit angert – an' my Fadder sed we sud nivver gang back again.'

So ended Betty Yewdale's account of her adventures with the 'terrible knitters' – a tag which the hard-working women of Dent must have found a little hard to live down, but which made an obvious title to the tale.

THE WALK:	MAP SQUARE: H5
AROUND DENT	National Grid Ref: SD 660887
	Leisurely stroll.

Uncompromisingly called Dent Town, in recognition of its ancient status as 'capital' of its own little valley, the picturesque village stands beyond the head of Wensleydale, a few miles south-east of Sedbergh. Its cobbled street winds past old limestone cottages beside the River Dee, and the fells rise on every side.

Dent is now mainly a farming community, but in its time it has been well known for cheese-making, quarrying and, of course, hand knitting. At the beginning of the nineteenth century, the hosiery masters at Kendal were said to collect 840 pairs of woollen stockings a week from Dent and Sedbergh, and in those days, Sedbergh was smaller and less important than Dent.

Near the church is a granite memorial in the form of a fountain

Cobbled street in Dent with the Sedgwick memorial.

to *Adam Sedgwick. Son of the vicar, and most famous son of Dent, Sedgwick was a pioneer geologist who became Professor of Geology at Cambridge. The church itself still has the initialled pews occupied by the old town's Statesmen in the seventeenth century.*

Dent Station, four miles east, is the highest main-line station in England.

LAKELAND FRINGES – WEST

The Luck of Muncaster

Buried Treasures

The Virgin Princess

32. THE LUCK OF MUNCASTER

A little to the east of Ravenglass is the beautifully situated Muncaster Castle, standing on a spur in the estuary of the River Esk. It was built originally around 1200, and has been almost entirely rebuilt in modern times, but it is the ancestral home of the Pennington family, whose head is Lord Muncaster. Among the treasures of the house is a glass drinking bowl, enamelled and gilded, which has been in the family's possession since 1463, when it was given to Sir John Pennington by King Henry VI. It is called the Luck of Muncaster.

During those years when the weak-minded and pious Lancastrian king had been deposed by his Yorkist rival, and his formidable queen Margaret of Anjou was temporarily in France, Henry himself hid for a time in Bywell Castle in Northumberland. When the final defeat came nearby, at the Battle of Hexham, the throneless king fled, and wandered

A view from Muncaster Castle.

about as a miserable fugitive until he was captured in 1465 and taken to London as a traitor.

In this period, in 1463, Henry was found by shepherds, wandering on Muncaster Fell, after apparently trying to gain admittance to Irton Hall, but being refused. The shepherds took him to Muncaster, where Sir John Pennington received him and gave him refuge. In return, as a stone in Muncaster church records: 'Holie Kinge Harrye gave Sir John a brauce wrkyd glass cuppe . . . whylles the familie shold keep hit unbrecken they shold gretely thryve.' And thrive they did, for their descendants and the unbroken cup are still there.

The Luck of Muncaster is one of a number of such 'lucks' or talismans recorded in Cumbria, and certainly, it would seem, one of the most effective. An equally well-known 'luck' was that of the Musgraves of Eden Hall, near Penrith. This one, according to tradition, was stolen from fairies, who chanted:

'If that glass should break or fall
Farewell the luck of Edenhall.'

Alas for the Musgraves, their luck ran out though they kept the glass intact, for the glass is now safe and sound in the Victoria and Albert Museum, but the Musgraves have gone and their mansion has been demolished.

The fact that most Cumbrian 'lucks' are associated with fairies or goblins, but not the Muncaster one, indicates the almost supernatural powers that were attributed to the 'holie' King Henry, who was shocked by the sight of a woman in a low-cut gown, and declared, when Margaret of Anjou presented him with a child, that it must be the son of the Holy Spirit! Perhaps Henry should have kept the Muncaster bowl himself. His own luck ran out eight years afterwards. After losing his wits, his son and his kingdoms of France and England, he finally lost his life in the Tower, leaving the Wars of the Roses as his legacy to his people.

THE WALK:
AROUND MUNCASTER
CASTLE AND GROUNDS

MAP SQUARE: C5
National Grid Ref: SD 097966
Stroll at leisure. Easy.

*A mile east of Ravenglass on the A595 you will find a car park on
the left, directly opposite the entrance to the castle grounds. You
will have to pay an entrance fee at the gates, but I recommend you
to do this, as both the grounds and the castle are well worth seeing,
particularly in spring when brilliant masses of rhododendron and
azalea are in bloom. There are fine views from the beautifully
laid-out gardens, and the castle itself contains some fine treasures.
A walk round this civilized spot makes an interesting change of
pace from the wilder scenes of other Lakeland walks.*

*There is a public right of way to the church a little farther along
the main road, on the right.*

33. BURIED TREASURES

You might with some justice call Borrowdale the Klondike of the Lake District and Ennerdale its Persian Gulf. Here is the whole story in black and white.

The precious metal that brought men prospecting to Borrowdale was not gold, but what the locals called 'wadd'. It was black-lead, or graphite – an ordinary enough substance, you might think, used in making lubricants and pencils. But at the end of the eighteenth century, at exactly the time when the Gold Rush was at its height in Canada, the wadd mines of Borrowdale had to be protected by armed guards and an Act of Parliament. The miners were searched before they left work, and the graphite had to be escorted on its journey to the industrial centres that used it.

Tales worthy of Will Ritson were told by old wives in the neighbourhood about the remarkable properties of the stuff. If you ground it into a paste and took a teaspoonful in a glass of white wine, it was supposed to be an infallible cure for all sorts of distemper, by causing sweating, urinating and vomiting. The cure sounds rather worse than the disease, but do-it-yourself physicians were not the only people to appreciate the value of the wadd. Farmers used it to brand their sheep; metal-workers used it as a protector against rust; cloth-dyers used it to make their colours fast. Another theory worthy of Auld Will was that the wadd was soot from the fires of hell, forced up to the earth's crust during Borrowdale's volcanic birth.

The natives of Borrowdale had known about the black-lead for ages, but it was only when the stuff was 'discovered' by capitalist landowners that the locals thought they might as well have a share of the profits, and started illicit mining, and smuggling the wadd out of the dale on packhorses, to Keswick or to the coast via Styhead.

The Lakeland geologist John Postlethwaite described the wadd – the purest graphite deposits in the world – as being in vertical pipes as much as sixty feet deep, and similar in formation to the diamond deposits in South Africa. One such 'pipe' found in 1803 yielded graphite worth over a hundred thousand pounds, and although the mines have long since been exhausted and closed, optimists still occasionally come to explore the diminutive slag-heaps in hopes of striking it rich in pencil lead.

Even more recent than the wadd-mining boom, however, was Lakeland's pearl-fishing craze, which reached its peak (understandably enough) during the General Strike in 1926. The 'pearl rush' was concentrated in the rivers of West Cumberland, particularly the Ehen, which flows from Ennerdale Water into the sea at Calder Hall.

British pearls, grown by freshwater mussels in the river

Ennerdale Water.

beds, were known to the Romans, and in medieval times the pearls, like the graphite, were held to be of medicinal value, ground to powder or even swallowed whole. Pearls have been found in the rivers of west Cumbria for centuries, and apart from being a fairly well-kept secret for obvious reasons, the beds have been protected by law from poachers. But it seems that a Londoner started the pearl rush of this century, by casually remarking in a public house in Ennerdale that he financed his holidays in the Lake District by selling the pearls he found. This story spread like wildfire, and soon the rivers were full of men, waist deep in the water, searching the beds for mussels whose shells might be miniature treasure chests.

Nowadays, of course, the river beds, like the wadd mines, are unproductive, and are in any case strictly controlled by the river authorities, but if you should happen to see a fellow in waders in one of the rivers of west Cumbria, you cannot always be sure that he is after trout or salmon.

THE WALK:	MAP SQUARE: C3
ENNERDALE WATER	National Grid Ref: NY 070159
	3¼ miles or 9 miles. Short walk
	easy: longer one a little difficult
	in places and not for the
	nervous.

Drive to the village of Ennerdale Bridge from Cleator Moor. The road crosses the River Ehen at Wath Brow, where some of the best pearl finds are said to have been made. The road then follows the course of the river, which is also the boundary of the National Park as far as Ennerdale Bridge. Park there and walk up the road towards Croasdale. After passing the wood on the right, a lane leaves the main road, on the right, and takes you down past How Hall Farm to the west short of Ennerdale Water.

This lake is one of the least visited in the district, because of its relative inaccessibility from the popular centres in central and eastern Lakeland, but it has plenty to offer the sightseer. It was called Broadwater at one time, and is flanked by crags and wooded fells.

If you are doing the short walk, turn right at the lake shore and walk along it until you see a hard track leaving it to the right. Follow this by the wall to the corner of a wood, then keep along the track as it passes between this wood and another on the right. Turn right at the T-junction, along the edge of the wood again, until you come to the road, where you turn left to get back to Ennerdale Bridge.

If you wish to do the long walk, right round the lake, turn left at the shore and simply follow the path and the road, which keep close to the lakeside except at the eastern end, where the road goes half a mile beyond the lake before you leave it by a track to cross the River Liza by a footbridge. Then the path returns to the head of the lake via a small wood, and goes back along the other side. The walk at the head of the lake is liable to be wet, and the return along the south shore rather rough going underfoot, particularly over the scree of Anglers Crag, where care is needed. Having negotiated this, however, you are nearly 'home'. Cross the river by the bridge near the Water Works Gauge House and continue along the shore until you come to a hard track off left by a wall. Follow this up between two woods to the T-junction, turn right, then left at the road, and you are shortly back in Ennerdale Bridge.

34. THE VIRGIN PRINCESS

The parish church of St Bees, which has – among other things – Cumbria's most spectacular Norman doorway, is dedicated to St Mary and St Bega, and it stands on the site of a seventh-century Benedictine nunnery, which St Bega founded.

Bega, we are told, was an Irish princess, the daughter of that island's monarch, and she had vowed to remain a virgin all her life. Her father, the king, however, was adamant that she was to marry a prince from Norway, and at last her only means of escaping the wedding was to flee the court, and she set sail alone, in a small boat, to cross the Irish Sea. But a wild storm blew up and drove the boat towards a dangerous headland on the Cumberland coast. In a prayer, Bega reaffirmed her vow, and asked God to save her life so that she could devote it to his service.

Landing safely in the sandstone bay below the cliffs, Bega took refuge in a cave to recover, and decided to live in a hermitage on the spot where she had been delivered from the storm. She went to the Lord of Egremont, who owned all the land in that region, and asked him to give her a small plot of land that she might live on. But the Baron only laughed at her, and said scornfully that he would give her as much land as was covered by snow on the following morning, which was Midsummer Day!

When he awoke, Lord Egremont was thunderstruck by the sight that greeted him when he looked out of his window. A great stretch of his land, three miles to the sea and along the coastline, was covered with snow. He kept his promise, and Bega founded a nunnery there. She also founded a harbour, for the safety of boats at sea, farther along the snow-covered coast. And that is how St Bees and Whitehaven came to be so named.

The original nunnery was destroyed by Viking invaders, then refounded after the Norman Conquest, and destroyed again at the Dissolution, but the dedication of the priory church remains as testimony to the Christian influence of the holy princess, St Bega the Virgin.

At St Bees Head.

THE WALK:
ALONG ST BEES HEAD

MAP SQUARE: A3
National Grid Ref: NY 971116
About 7 miles. A little care needed at the beginning, and rather steep in places. Not for anyone who is afraid of heights.

Park in the sandstone village of St Bees and look at the church first, then walk to the beach. Turning right along the shoreline, walk to the end of the beach and follow the footpath up the cliff with the fence on your right. (There are moments when you might wish the fence was on your left.) Below these cliffs, where St Bega is supposed to have landed, there is now an important seabird colony, with puffins, guillemots, fulmars and razorbills, among others.

Continue along the clifftop path until you come to the lighthouse, which is 99 feet high. The path may be slippery if wet. If it is a clear day, you may be able to see the Scottish and Irish coasts, as well as the Isle of Man. Go on past the lighthouse, following the path down into a gulley and up through a stile in the fence, going alongside the fence until you come to a wall. Turn right, away from the coast, and go through a gate to a lane. Whitehaven is not a pretty sight, but you will soon be walking away from it. Turn left at the crossroads and go along the road until you reach a right turn on to a stony lane. Bear left past some cottages and continue to the main road. Turning right, walk along this quiet road beside a brook, through Rottington village, and continue back to St Bees.

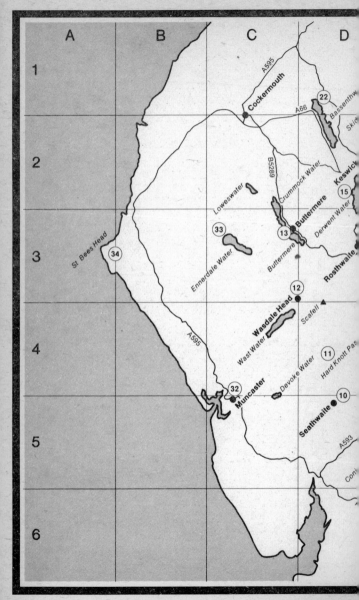

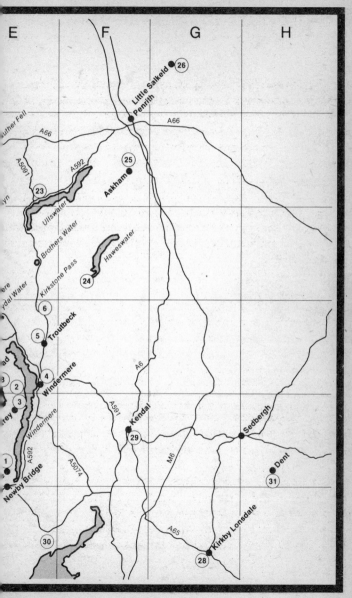

KEY TO REFERENCE MAP